LIVING WITH
PURPOSE
BIBLE STUDY

Romans

LIVING WITH
PURPOSE
BIBLE STUDY

Romans

Guideposts

A Gift from Guideposts

Thank you for your purchase! We want to express our gratitude for your support with a special gift just for you.

Dive into *Spirit Lifters*, a complimentary e-book that will fortify your faith, offering solace during challenging moments. Its 31 carefully selected scripture verses will soothe and uplift your soul.

Please use the QR code or go to **guideposts.org/ spiritlifters** to download.

Living with Purpose Bible Study: Romans

Published by Guideposts
100 Reserve Road, Suite E200
Danbury, CT 06810
Guideposts.org

Cover design by Judy Ross
Interior design by Judy Ross
Cover photo by Jertography/Getty Images
Typeset by Aptara, Inc.

ISBN 978-1-961251-37-3 (hardcover)
ISBN 978-1-961251-24-3 (softcover)
ISBN 978-1-961251-39-7 (ebook)

Printed and bound in the United States of America
10 9 8 7 6 5 4 3 2 1

CONTENTS

About Living with Purpose Bible Study

For as long as humankind has existed, we have pondered our place in the universe. Poets and preachers, philosophers and scientists alike have explored the topic for generations. Our busy modern lives leave little time for contemplation, and yet we move through our lives with nagging questions in the back of our minds: *Why am I here? What am I meant to do with my life?*

Fyodor Dostoevsky wrote that the "mystery of human existence lies not in just staying alive, but in finding something to live for." You might wonder how living with purpose ties in with the Bible. That's because God's Word is a guidebook for life, and God Himself has a purpose—a unique mission—for and unique to you. Reading the Bible and seeking God through prayer are two of the main ways God speaks to people. And when we begin to seek God, when we pursue His truth, when we begin to live our lives in ways that reflect His love back to others, we begin to find that purpose. Finding our purpose is not a destination; it is a journey we'll travel until we leave this earth behind and go to our heavenly Father.

Most of us know something about the Bible. We might be able to quote verses that we memorized as kids. Many of us have read parts of it, have learned about it in Sunday school both as children and adults. But not as many of us *know* the Bible, and that is where this Bible study comes in.

"Bible study" is a term that can elicit a variety of responses. For some people, the feeling that comes is a daunting sense of intimidation, even fear, because we worry that the Bible will somehow find us wanting, less than, rejected. Maybe we've heard preachers wielding the Bible as a weapon, using it as a measuring rod and a dividing line that separates "us" from "them."

Guideposts' *Living with Purpose Bible Study* addresses these questions and concerns with a hope-filled, welcoming, inclusive voice, like the one you've grown to know and love from Guideposts' devotional books, story collections, magazines, and website.

Best of all, you'll discover that the writers of *Living with Purpose Bible Study* are experts not only in the depth of their Bible knowledge but also in sharing that knowledge in such a welcoming, winning way that you can't help but be drawn in.

The writers come alongside you as trusted friends, guiding you through each volume in that warm, inviting manner that only Guideposts could bring you.

Each volume in the study draws from five trusted translations of the Bible: the New International Version, New American Standard Bible, the Amplified Version, the English Standard Version, and the King James Version of the Bible. We encourage you to keep your favorite Bible translation on hand as you read each study chapter. The Bible passages you read act as the foundation from which the study writer's insights, information, and inspiration flow. You can read along with the writers as each chapter unfolds, or you can read all of the passages or verses included in the chapter prior to reading it. It's up to you; you can use the method that works best for you.

In addition, you'll find two distinct features to enhance your experience: "A Closer Look" entries bring context by presenting historical, geographical, or cultural information, and "Inspiration from Romans" entries demonstrate the spiritual insights people like you have gained from their knowledge of the biblical text. We've also provided lined writing spaces at the end of each lesson for you to jot down your own thoughts, questions, discoveries, and *aha* moments that happen as you read and study.

A final note: Before you read each chapter, we encourage you to pray, asking that God will open your eyes and heart to what He has to say. Our prayer for you is that you find a new or renewed sense of purpose and grow closer to God as you deepen your understanding of God's Word by enjoying this *Living with Purpose Bible Study*.

—*The Editors of Guideposts*

An Overview of Romans

The Greatest Letter Ever Written

The book of Romans is profound and life changing. To give us an idea of how much influence Paul's letter to the Romans has had on our world and on history, it is helpful to look at how it transformed some of the people who, in turn, transformed the world, changing the course of human history forever.

It was after reading two verses in Romans (13:13–14) that Augustine returned to the faith of his mother, Monica, and to the faith of his own childhood—a faith he had deserted as a young man. Following his baptism on Easter Sunday AD 387, Augustine dedicated himself to a life of study and became, other than Paul, probably the greatest theologian and defender of the faith in the history of the Christian church.

In AD 1515 a deeply troubled monk named Martin Luther was reflecting on the opening chapter of Romans when the truth of these words penetrated his mind and heart for the first time: "For therein is the righteousness of God revealed from faith to faith: as it is written, The just shall live by faith" (1:17, KJV). Out of that discovery the Protestant Reformation was born. Luther later wrote, "This letter is truly the most important piece in the New Testament. It is the purest Gospel."

Some two hundred years later, in 1732, a spiritually unsettled clergyman in the Church of England attended a meeting in Aldersgate Street in London and heard a layman read Luther's Preface to the Epistle to the Romans. After hearing this reading, John Wesley wrote in his journal, "About a quarter before nine while he was describing the change which God works in the heart through faith in Christ, I felt my heart strangely warmed." Paul's words lit a flame that night that moved across England and then to America and throughout the world in the form of the great Methodist movement.

Samuel Taylor Coleridge, famed English poet, critic, and philosopher, may have expressed it best in 1833 when he said, "I think St. Paul's Epistle to the Romans the most profound work in existence."[1]

Other luminaries of history and the Christian faith were also profoundly influenced by Romans, such as Thomas Aquinas; William Tyndale; John Calvin; Karl Barth; theologian, writer, and martyr Dietrich Bonhoeffer, as well as his fiancée, Maria von Wedemeyer, who, after Bonhoeffer's execution, continued to live a life of faith and service, embodying the principles they both cherished; and, finally, Pakistani-American author and speaker Bilquis Sheikh, for whom Romans 9:25–26 was instrumental in her conversion and who went on to give her testimony around the United States and the world. These are just some of those whose lives were

---

[1] *The Complete Works of Samuel Taylor Coleridge* (Volume 6): "Virtue and Liberty—Epistle to the Romans-Erasmus—Luther," June 15, 1833. Professor Shedd, editor. Harper & Brothers, New York. https://www.google.com/books/edition/The_Complete_Works_of_Samuel_Taylor_Cole/Bg2aAAAAIAAJ?hl=en&gbpv=1&dq=%22I+think+St.+Paul%27s+Epistle+to+the+Romans+the+most+profound+work+in+existence%22+samuel+coleridge+taylor&pg=PA458&printsec=frontcover.

changed by their study of Romans and in turn changed the world and the church through thoughts, words, and actions that sent ripples across the fabric of human history.

From the earliest days of the church, Christians have treasured Paul's Epistle to the Romans as one of the clearest and finest statements of faith ever written. It is in this letter that Paul, the learned apostle to the Gentiles, spelled out in straightforward and simple language his detailed understanding of the Good News of Jesus Christ.

The Background of Paul's Letter

Paul did not bring the gospel to the church in Rome. While we don't know for sure just how or when this happened, Paul was very much aware of the Christian fellowship there. In fact, even though he had not visited Rome, he had many friends in that church. These were people he had no doubt known in Asia Minor and Greece who had moved to Rome.

It was to these first-generation Christians—some with a Jewish heritage but mostly Gentiles—that Paul wrote the words we turn our attention to now. The Gospels and Acts were largely narrative, but now the pace and tone of our New Testament change.

In Romans, following his introduction (1:1–17), Paul moves on to discuss the universal need for salvation and explains that it comes by being made right before God through faith in Jesus Christ (1:19–4:25). Then from 5:1 to 8:39 we learn the consequences, or results, of salvation. And from 9:1 to 11:36 Paul writes specifically about the relationship between the Jews and Christ.

Ranging from 12:1 to 15:13 we have a profound statement of Christlike behavior. Here Paul speaks to how the Roman Christians and we, as sons and daughters of God and as a church fellowship, are to act and relate to one another.

And finally, from 15:14 to 16:27 we have Paul's conclusion to the letter—his plans and reasons for writing, his personal greetings, and his closing prayer of benediction.

Throughout our study together we will learn much about the problems that confronted first-century Christians—some only recently converted from paganism—and first-century churches. At the same time, we see an interesting parallel between their problems and ours. When Paul pleads for unity, for a spirit of love and appreciation for each other, for patience and under-standing, it is almost as if he were speaking to our deepest needs today. And when he calls for his readers to behave and act each day in a manner as Christlike as their words of witness, we get the haunting feeling that Paul is writing to us.

The Circumstances behind Paul's Letter

When we move along in the New Testament from the four Gospels and the Acts of the Apostles to the Epistle to the Romans, we abruptly come to an entirely new type of litera-ture. Though it might sound formal and lofty to our modern ears, the word *epistle* is simply another word for "letter," and that is exactly what Romans is.

The book of Acts, like the Gospels before it (except John), was written in the form of a historical narrative—it tells a story. Romans and the next twenty books of the New Testament, however, do not tell stories; they are examples of the correspondence written by Paul and other Early Church leaders to congregations and sometimes to individuals who needed encouragement, instruction, and guidance—in a word, discipling.

Students of the New Testament often refer to these letters as *occasional* literature, which can sound odd to our ears. In this context, occasional means that each of these letters was written on a specific occasion and to meet a specific need. Certain writers wrote to churches or people in particular places at distinct times about issues that confronted those Christians. If we are to fully appreciate the meaning of these letters, we need to understand the circumstances surrounding them. The letters in the New Testament can become more meaningful for us when we understand the occasions that prompted them.

Let's focus our attention on the letters of Paul. Some features of the life situations of each letter are common to several of the letters, and sometimes to all of them. Others are peculiar to that individual letter. Obviously, for example, all of these letters are attributed to Paul and are often referred to as the Pauline Epistles. Some, such as the letters written while Paul was in prison—Ephesians, Philippians, Colossians, and Philemon—share a common place and approximately the same time of writing. Yet for the most part, his other letters were written from different locations and at different points in time in his missionary career.

To understand the letters, then, we need to know something of *Paul's personal circumstances* at the time he wrote each one. Moreover, all of the letters addressed to churches were written to congregations about whom Paul was especially concerned. Most of them were sent to churches that Paul had founded. But two of them—Romans and Colossians—were written to congregations that he had neither founded nor visited. For this reason, the nature of his concern for each of these churches was quite distinctive. Consequently, we need to know about the *situation confronting each church* in order to understand Paul's response to each congregation.

Since all of Paul's letters in our Bible today have come down to us from the earliest days of the church as sacred writings and still speak authoritatively to men and women today, we sometimes overlook the historical circumstances in which they were written. We look at each one as addressing the same situation: *our situation.* Certainly these documents contain timeless truths that apply just as much to our time as they did to those first Christian readers. But we should never forget that these truths were first stated in very definite historical circumstances.

Obviously, then, for us to find the fullest meaning of the timeless truths in Paul's letters, we must understand the circumstances that caused Paul to write them. As a matter of fact, it is only when we understand Paul's message *within* its original setting that we have a basis for applying that message to our situation. Let us look then at the circumstances associated with the Epistle to the Romans.

Paul's Personal Situation

Paul's third missionary journey was coming to a close. Having begun this phase of his work with an overland journey from

Palestine across Asia Minor, Paul had concentrated his efforts in the coastal city of Ephesus for three years. Now, with a desire to move on to other areas that had not yet heard the gospel, the apostle had decided to leave this city where he had served longer than any other place in his missionary career.

Before returning to Jerusalem, though, he felt the need to revisit churches that he had founded and worked with in earlier travels around the Aegean basin (Acts 20:1–2). As indicated elsewhere in the book of Acts, Paul had returned repeatedly to the churches he had established to encourage and strengthen the fledgling congregations. Such visits seem to have been a vital part of his strategy. In fact, it often appears that the letters he wrote were substitutes for visits that he was prevented from making because of imprisonments or pressing needs in the communities in which he was then working.

But there was another reason for the return visits this time. Although not explicitly mentioned in Acts, this reason is indicated in three of Paul's letters (1 Corinthians 16:1 and following; 2 Corinthians 9:1 and following; Romans 15:25 and following). He was returning to these Gentile churches to pick up the offering they had collected for the impoverished saints—believers—in the Jerusalem church, a poverty brought about by a long season of famine in the area during that time.

Concerned about two factions in the Early Church—the Jewish Christians and the Gentile Christians—Paul saw in this offering a possibility for breaching the gap that existed between these two groups. After all, he thought, the Gentiles were indebted to the Jews within the church, for it was through the Jews that the gospel had first been brought to the

Gentile world. Now if the Gentile churches sent money to the impoverished Jewish Christians in Jerusalem, they would feel a sense of indebtedness to the Gentiles. What better way to resolve differences than to foster a feeling of mutual indebtedness or mutual interdependence!

Thus Paul had left Ephesus, visited the churches of Macedonia, and was now in Greece on the last leg of his collection ministry. Since Gaius is mentioned as Paul's host (16:23), and Corinth is where Paul baptized a man by the same name (see also 1 Corinthians 1:14), Corinth is usually assumed to be the place where Paul wrote his epistle to the Romans.

Why, then, would he at this point in his career write this lengthiest of all his letters to a church he had neither founded nor visited up to that time? First, he was concerned about his upcoming reception in Jerusalem. This city that stood at the heart of Judaism potentially held very real danger for him. In Jerusalem there were many who wished him harm because he, a former champion of Judaism and fanatical persecutor of the church, had converted to Christianity.

Furthermore, he was uncertain about the possible reaction of the Christian Jews to the gift he was bringing from the Gentiles. Would it be received in the spirit of love and unity with which it was sent? Would it bond these differing groups together? Or would it be viewed with mistrust and resentment and drive a deeper wedge between the two groups?

So Paul wrote to the Romans to solicit their prayer support. As he faced his adversaries and delivered the collection, he wanted to be assured that Christians in Rome were praying for him (15:31). Just as names of missionaries today are circulated among Christians who don't know them personally but are willing to pray for them and their work, Paul in the first century was sending his requests for prayer to a church that did not know him.

Paul also had another request in mind. He had decided that his work in Ephesus was now completed (15:23), and he was looking forward to a new field of service. But his intention was not an extended ministry in Rome; instead, he intended to go to Spain (15:24, 28). Paul was attracted to places that had never heard the gospel (15:20). In modern vernacular, he was a church *planter*; his gift was in starting new works.

Confident that others could build upon the foundation he had laid in Ephesus, Paul was now ready to begin again in Spain. As soon as he had delivered the Gentile Christians' gift to the church in Jerusalem, he would head west. Between Jerusalem and Spain, however, lay Rome, the magnificent capital city that he had never visited. There was also a thriving church in Rome about which Paul had heard much but seen nothing. A visit with these Roman Christians would provide not only an opportunity for fellowship and mutual encouragement but also a possible source of financial support for the western enterprise.

Although Paul did not normally anticipate financial aid from the churches that he had founded (see also 1 Corinthians 9:12–15), he would have no qualms about soliciting and accepting such help from the Roman Christians. He had not founded their church! To be sure, he would not directly ask them for such resources in this letter, but he would drop a hint. He would indicate his hope that, after visiting with the

Romans, he would be sped on his journey to Spain by them (Romans 15:24).

One could say that Paul wrote this letter to solicit the Romans' support, both in prayer and in financial resources, for his mission enterprise. These requests perhaps explain the curious fact that this letter, the longest Paul ever wrote, was written to a congregation that he had never seen. In a way, he was writing a letter of self-introduction, establishing his credentials, and identifying those ideas that he and they held in common, in order to demonstrate to them that he was worthy of their trust and partnership in the spreading of the gospel.

The Situation of the Roman Church

As the capital of a sprawling empire that circled the Mediterranean Sea, Rome was the most important city in the first-century world. From its gates, soldiers had gone out to conquer and thereby form the most impressive empire the western world had ever seen. To its colonnaded streets came peoples of all classes, occupations, religions, and cultures to be molded into a truly cosmopolitan community. With a population of well over a million people, it was the unrivaled center of urban culture in a world dominated by its political strength and its military might.

No one knows how the church at Rome was started or who started it. Although early Christian tradition indicates that both Peter and Paul died in Rome, the church in that city seems to have been thriving before either one of them arrived there. Perhaps it was established by Roman Jews who were converted to Christianity at Pentecost (see Acts 2:10) who then brought the Good News of Jesus Christ home with them.

It is uncertain just how Gentiles from the city were added to their number. It is known, though, that Jews in general, or perhaps Jewish Christians in particular, were driven from the city by the edict of the emperor Claudius about the year AD 49 (see Acts 18:2). Any Christians who were left must have been Gentile. Presumably, after the death of Claudius in AD 54, Jewish Christians were able to return to their former home. Though they had once been the backbone of the Roman church, the Jews came back to a congregation that was thoroughly Gentile. Moreover, just as problems had emerged in other areas between Gentiles and Jews within the same churches, difficulties also began to arise here. One group, calling themselves the "strong," was acting in a judgmental manner toward those whom they considered weak (see Romans 14:1–15:13). Such divisions had the potential of disrupting or even destroying the fellowship.

The Roman Christians were ready for some apostolic advice, and Paul was ready to give it. Even though he had not founded the church, he thought it appropriate to give apostolic counsel to the congregation. After all, he was the apostle to the Gentiles (Galatians 2:7). And since they were predominantly Gentile, they fell within his sphere of influence.

Paul wrote to the Romans, then, not just to solicit *their* support but to offer *his* support to them. He wrote so that he and they might be mutually edified.

Why Study Romans?

The book of Romans has been universally recognized over the centuries as the most significant theological document ever written. This evaluation has been based on several observations.

First, no Christian thinker has been more important or influential than Paul. Thirteen of the twenty-seven books of the New Testament are attributed to him. Although he wasn't the first missionary, certainly none in the first century or in any century since has contributed more to the spread of the gospel than he did. Primarily because of Paul, Christianity was transformed from a Palestinian Jewish sect into a religious movement of worldwide significance.

Second, Romans was to some extent a letter of self-introduction. So instead of devoting his attention to the concerns of a particular congregation as he did in 1 Corinthians, Paul in Romans taught certain themes that were central to his own Christian faith. To be sure, he did not produce an exhaustive digest of all his beliefs—he did not even mention the Lord's Supper, for example—but he did write the most fully developed presentation that we have of his understanding of the Christian faith.

With its deep dive into doctrine, Romans might at first feel intimidating, but it is worth our effort to study it. The overarching message of Romans is the importance of faith and an understanding of the transcendent peace, the immeasurable grace, and the hope of glory that we experience through faith in Him. Granted, in the first part of his letter, Paul lays down the law and outlines the fact that our falling short of it—sin—is what makes salvation necessary. But he then goes on to provide the antidote to sin, which is given freely for the asking (see Romans 3:24): grace through faith in Jesus Christ.

Getting to know Paul and coming face-to-face with his spiritual experiences and wisdom is indeed a life-changing experience. So get yourself a cup of coffee or tea, open your favorite Bible to the book of Romans, and make yourself comfortable as we delve into this stirring letter together.

The Theme of the Epistle: Justification by Faith

Lord, help me to not only understand this lesson but also allow it to bear fruit in my life. AMEN.

Greetings

Most of us write our letters in a rather standard form. At the head we usually put our return address, the date, and a greeting or salutation. Following the body of the letter, we close with a suitable word or two—sincerely yours, cordially yours—and then add our signature.

In the first century, the pattern was somewhat different, and Paul conformed to the custom of that time (1:1–7). The pattern then was to begin the letter with the name of the sender. This was followed by the name of the recipient and a formal greeting. Although the arrangement seems strange to us, imagine how convenient it was for the reader. Since letters were written on scrolls—some could be as long as thirty feet!—it was helpful for the name of the sender to be given first. The reader did not have to unroll the whole scroll to see who was writing. Although Paul does conform to the pattern of the day, he infuses these rather routine elements with significant theological insights.

As a rule, Paul identified himself with one or two words or phrases. But since he is writing to people who do not know him, he gives a longer self-introduction (1:1–6).

Of course, the first word of identification that he gives is his own name. Paul is not the name by which the apostle is first mentioned in the New Testament. In the book of Acts, he is first introduced as Saul of Tarsus. As a matter of fact, many people suggest that his own conversion to Christianity had such a profound impact on him that it even changed his name from Saul to Paul! In Acts, however, after his conversion, he is still called Saul in chapters 9–13. It is not until the first missionary journey is well underway that the name Paul is introduced (Acts 13:9).

More than likely the man was given *both* names at birth. His parents were not only good Jews but also Roman citizens. They probably gave their son a familiar Jewish name, Saul, as well as a good Roman name, Paul. An exact parallel to this is the double name of one of Paul's traveling companions: John (Jewish) Mark (Greco-Roman). In Paul's earlier life as a devout Jew in Jerusalem, he would have been called by his Jewish name. But when his life became centered on the mission to the Gentiles, his Roman name was predominantly used. For this reason, he identified himself as Paul in this letter since it was addressed primarily to Gentile Christians.

In addition to his name, three key ideas are found in verse 1: Paul says that he is a servant, an apostle, and one set apart. His use of the word *servant* (NIV, KJV)—but also translated "slave" or "bond-servant" in some translations—would at first seem strange to any Gentile reader. The idea of servanthood or slavery was abhorrent to them, but Paul wanted them to fully understand that he belonged completely to Christ. And so, without hesitation, he refers to himself as a servant to underline his commitment.

In all his letters Paul identifies himself as "apostle." The term means "one sent out." Borrowed from the language of diplomacy, this word originally indicated one who was commissioned or sent out as an official representative of another. The word was used, for example, to describe the person sent as an envoy from one king to the court of another. It was also used to describe someone who was commissioned by a king to go out to accomplish a specific task. Such a person had no authority of his own. All authority rested with the one who had done the sending.

Paul felt that he had been commissioned by God to accomplish a specific task. He was God's representative as he proclaimed the gospel to the Gentiles. "Apostle" was a cherished word for him. It did not suggest that he exercised his own authority. Rather it indicated that he was God's representative. By using the term, Paul was not calling attention to himself; his emphasis was on the One who had commissioned him.

Paul's appointment had come from God, who had "separated" or set him apart. It has been suggested that the term "Pharisee" also comes from this same root word. The Pharisees, including Saul of Tarsus, were those who thought that they, because of their rigid observance of the Law, had separated themselves from ordinary or common people. There was a smugness about their self-separation.

But Paul's separation was different. He had not separated himself from others. It was God who had set him apart. In fact, he had not been separated *from* anyone. Rather he had been separated *for* a purpose: to proclaim the gospel, the Good News of what God has accomplished in Jesus Christ.

By mentioning the word *gospel*, Paul uses a word that establishes a rapport with his readers. They have been transformed by this same Good News. Convinced that the Christ event is the fulfillment of Old Testament hopes, "which He promised beforehand through His prophets in the holy Scriptures" (1:2, NASB), Paul defines the content of the gospel in the next two verses (1:3–4) by citing what was perhaps a primitive confession of faith concerning Jesus.

Two very important facts about Jesus are mentioned in these two verses. First, Paul says that Jesus was "descended from David according to the flesh" (1:3, ESV). This statement further enforces what Paul has already written in verse 2, that Jesus had come in fulfillment of Old Testament expectations.

Second, Paul writes that Jesus was "declared to be the Son of God *with power,* according to the spirit of holiness, by the resurrection from the dead" (1:4, KJV; italics added for emphasis). Paul isn't saying here that Jesus only became the Son of God at the Resurrection, but that He became the *Son of God with power* at the Resurrection. This event was the beginning of His reign as exalted Lord, in contrast with His apparent weakness as a human being. As a matter of fact, it was only after the Resurrection that this One who was descended from David was actually recognized and worshipped as the Son of God.

After making it clear who Jesus is, Paul returns to his self-introduction in verse 5 and says that it is this exalted Son of God who has called him to be an apostle. Specifically, his commission is to bring about the "obedience to the faith," the positive response of faith to the gospel, "among all nations" (1:5, KJV). (The Greek word translated "nations" can also be translated as "Gentiles.") Among this large group are Paul's readers (1:6). Paul then strengthens the bond between them and himself by saying that they too have been called by God, just as he has been called to be an apostle.

The word *called* in verse 6 is a transition to the next part of the salutation of the letter—the name of those who are receiving it. And these are the ones in Rome who are "loved by God and called to be saints" (1:7, ESV).

The term *saints* is often misunderstood by many modern Christians. We tend to think of a saint as an unusually pious Christian who is much holier than those of us who are ordinary members of the church. Usually we think of a saint as someone who lived a long time ago and is now dead. Is that not what we imply when we pay someone the ultimate compliment by saying, "She's a living saint"? In actuality, the word *saint* in the New Testament means "one who is made holy," and indeed the New International Version uses the term "his holy people" in verse 7. And for Paul, every Christian is a saint. Nowhere is this more obvious than in 1 Corinthians 1:2, where he uses the term to describe the Christians in that immature and problem-filled church.

Paul's actual greeting, "grace and peace" (1:7 in most translations), combines forms of two words of greeting used by the Greeks and Jews of the first century. "Grace" translates a Greek word whose original meaning had to do with that which was beautiful to behold. This idea is still preserved in our word "graceful." For the Greeks the word took on an additional meaning: "a gift of the gods." Someone was beautiful to behold only if the gods had bestowed that quality upon him or her. Paul seized upon that word as an apt summary of the gospel: the favor of God freely given to unworthy people. Here he used it not only as a greeting but also as a prayer for his readers.

"Shalom," a greeting used by Jews to this day, means "peace." But this term implies more than just the absence of warfare. In the New Testament it is used to describe the tranquil and stable relationship that exists between a person and God as a result of the reconciliation of God with mankind that was accomplished in Jesus Christ. This combination of Greek and Hebrew terms is used by Paul in all of his letters, and they are always listed in the same order: grace and peace. For Paul, no one can know real peace until he has accepted the grace that God offers.

Prayer of Thanksgiving

Again following the usual pattern of polite first-century Greco-Roman letters, Paul includes a prayer of thanksgiving for the readers after the greeting (1:8–15). He thanks God that the faith of the Roman Christians "is spoken of throughout the whole world" (1:8, KJV). Although he may be referring here to the depth or the strength of their faith, it is possible he meant nothing more than that there were people of faith, i.e., Christians, in the Roman capital.

Next Paul indicates the frequency of his prayers for the Romans: "Without ceasing I mention you always in my prayers" (1:9–10, ESV). The prayer of thanksgiving in this letter is not just a formality; it is an example of his repeated mention of the Roman Christians in his prayers. Even though he doesn't know them, he knows about them, and they are objects of his prayerful concern.

Paul then shares the content of his prayers with them: He prays that he might be able to visit them (1:10–14). We have already seen that Paul, as apostle to the Gentiles, felt that the predominantly Gentile church in Rome was within his area of responsibility. Even though the congregation was not started by him, nor did he normally want to build on another's foundation, a visit by Paul to the Romans could be mutually beneficial. Not only would he impart some spiritual gift or blessing to them (1:11), but he himself would be strengthened and comforted (encouraged) by them (1:12).

The giving and receiving of encouragement is never a one-direction procedure for a Christian. One person does not do all the giving while another does all the receiving. For Paul, a visit with the Roman Christians would be a time of mutual giving and receiving. They and he would be blessed by each other's encouragement.

Paul next tells them that often "I planned many times to come to you," but he had been prevented from doing so (1:13, NIV). Illness and adversity (see 2 Corinthians 11:23–27 for a list of obstacles he had endured) as well as pressing needs in other churches where he was working thwarted his earlier plans for a trip to Rome.

Next Paul tells why he wants to visit them: "in order that I might have a harvest among you" (1:13, NIV). We are inclined sometimes to think that Paul's only concern was the winning of converts. But if people have already been won to Christ in Rome and Paul still anticipates some harvest among them, he must think that nurture, as well as evangelism, is a worthy goal of his labors.

Paul now defines for his readers the extent of his work and mission among the Gentiles. He is "obligated" (verse 14, NIV) both to the Greeks (Greek-speaking people) and the barbarians (those who did not speak Greek), both to the wise (the educated) and the unwise (the uneducated). With these two pairs of contrasting terms, Paul made it clear that his work and ministry are for all Gentiles. He owes something to them all: the Good News about Jesus Christ. And since the Romans fit within these limits, he also wants to preach the gospel to them (1:15).

Statement of the Theme

Although this gospel, the Good News about Jesus Christ, may be seen as something foolish to the Greeks and weak to the Jews (see 1 Corinthians 1:23), Paul is not ashamed of it. With his usual candor, Paul states boldly, "For I am not ashamed of the gospel, for it is the power of God for salvation to everyone who believes, to the Jew first and also to the Greek" (1:16, ESV).

Paul is saying that instead of weakness or folly, the gospel is power—the potent ability to transform through salvation everyone who believes, who has faith. Furthermore, this power is available to everyone. Here Paul uses another pair of contrasting terms to make an inclusive statement: This salvation is for everyone—both Jew, to whom, historically, the gospel was first preached, and Greek (non-Jew) alike. But this salvation becomes operable only through belief, or faith.

Faith, for Paul, is not something a person does to earn salvation; it implies no meritorious effort on our part. From start to finish, salvation is an accomplishment of God; it is what He does for us. Faith, then, is the means by which we receive what God offers. Rather than an act, it is an attitude of openness or surrender to God. It marks the cessation of activity or effort on our part so that God can act in us, on us, for us. Faith is the response of our openness to God.

Paul now explains that it is in the gospel of Christ that the "righteousness of God" is revealed (1:17, NASB). Again we have one of those unusual terms in the Greek text that is translated by two different nouns in English: *righteousness* and *justification*. Incidentally, the corresponding adjective in Greek can also be translated both ways ("just" or "righteous"), as can the verb ("to justify" or "to make right"). Both ideas are important to Paul. Righteousness here is associated with God. Perhaps our first inclination is to see the idea as descriptive of God's nature; we can say, "God is righteous," in much the same way we might say, "God is holy." But we err if we limit the meaning of the term to a quality or an attribute of God. The word also points to His *activity*. God makes us righteous.

Many people have looked to the court of law concept of acquittal as providing the proper background for understanding the meaning of the term "righteousness" here. Implied is the notion that God acquits us even when we are guilty. He justifies us; He calls us *right.*

But to understand what is meant here we need to look at the root meaning of the word. Originally, the word had the idea of putting someone or something into the right way. It is not just *calling* someone right, but it is actually *making* a person right! For example, let's say that you notice that one of the books on your shelves has fallen over. Instead of standing upright, it is lying flat. Now the book could try all day to right itself, to put itself back into the upright position, but that it cannot do. It doesn't have the ability to make itself right again. That action can only be done by *someone* to the book.

When you see that book lying flat, you don't simply "call" it upright when it is not; you must actually make it right by putting it into its proper position. This kind of activity is what Paul had in mind when he used this term in reference to God. When there is absolutely nothing we can do for ourselves, God enters the picture and puts us into the proper position. *God actually* makes *people right!*

Paul says that this activity of God is revealed in the gospel, but the action becomes effective for the individual only by faith. In fact, he says, God's righteousness is revealed "from faith to faith" (1:17, NASB). This curious phrase might simply mean that this activity of God is a faith proposition from beginning to end. Or another possible meaning is that the first "faith" belongs to God and the second faith to an individual person. But in what sense can we say that God has faith?

The meaning may come clear for us when we remember that the term for "faith" here can also mean "belief"—"from belief to belief." The idea would be that God believes in us even before we believe in Him. This seems to agree with what Paul has said about grace. God initiates the process of salvation. To use a modern phrase, He offers us salvation "in good faith." Because He has faith in us, we can have faith in Him.

God offers, but He does not coerce. To be made right, we must accept what God offers to us. Paul then refers to a statement from the Old Testament prophet Habakkuk (2:4), which he quotes with new emphasis. The familiar translation, "The just shall live by faith" (verse 17, KJV), might better and more properly read, "The one who has been justified (made right) by faith shall live." Paul is not just describing a quality that characterizes the lifestyle of the person who is made just or righteous by God. Rather he is emphasizing here the means by which the person is made righteous—by faith.

With these words, Paul has given us the theme that he will develop in the remainder of the epistle. As a matter of fact, the theme, "justification by faith," characterizes Paul's theology better than any other descriptive phrase. Put simply: We are made right by God because of our response to God's offer of grace.

◆———————————————◆

Heavenly Father, thank You for justifying me,
for seeing me as clean. AMEN.

For I long to visit you so I can bring you some spiritual gift that will help you grow strong in the Lord. When we get together, I want to encourage you in your faith, but I also want to be encouraged by yours.

—Romans 1:11–12 (NLT)

Hoping to delay spinal surgery, my doctor connected me with a physical therapist who recommended modified exercises to strengthen my core muscles. Since I had planned to leave town for two weeks, I put off starting the program. Then I needed a week to unpack when I returned. I kept thinking of other reasons to procrastinate. Suddenly it was time for an appointment with the physical therapist—to measure how much progress I had made.

I also procrastinate when it comes to spiritual exercises, like Bible reading, prayer, and personal worship. God has provided tools and resources to help us strengthen our faith, grow in godliness, and prepare ourselves to serve Him faithfully. Inconsistency or neglect in these areas can leave us weak and stunt our spiritual growth. But until I read Romans 1, I hadn't thought about how my failure to stay spiritually fit affects others as well as myself.

We were created to "do life" together with other Christ followers, helping each other stay strong and grow deeper in the faith. We don't have to be a pastor or leader to do that. Words of encouragement at just the right time. Spurring someone on to fully use their spiritual gifts. Sharing words from the Bible that speak to someone's struggle. Extending practical help during difficult times. Or, maybe offering a listening ear and a warm hug. Basically, just sharing Jesus.

To think that I might help someone else grow stronger in their faith—what a sacred privilege!

—*Dianne Neal Matthews*

Notes

Notes

Notes

The Human Plight: Universal Need for Salvation

God, reveal to me anew Your blessing of salvation. Amen.

In summers throughout the 1950s, the excitement of school vacation was not the only emotion running high. People were also full of apprehension, for the warm months brought increased incidence of polio—infantile paralysis. Each day the newspapers recorded the growing numbers of victims who had fallen prey to this crippling disease. Then Dr. Jonas Salk created a vaccine that was so effective polio was all but eradicated.

In a real sense, only those who can remember the cruel reality of polio can fully appreciate the vaccine that eradicated it. Paul must have made a similar observation as he sat down to write his letter to the Romans. He wanted to express his understanding of the gospel, the Good News of what God had accomplished through Jesus Christ. But they could not fully appreciate the meaning of salvation without remembering the plight from which they had been saved. It was for this reason that Paul began his discussion with the basics—the predicament from which humankind needed to be delivered: universal sinfulness.

Paul's thought here seems to be easily divided into three main sections. First, he addresses the failings of the Gentiles (1:18–32). Next, he points out the problem of the Jews (2:1–3:8). And finally, he summarizes the predicament of people everywhere by acknowledging the fact of universal sinfulness and the need for salvation (3:9–20).

The Failings of the Gentiles (1:18–32)

When Paul said in verse 16 that God's salvation is available for everyone who believes, he specified "to the Jew first and also to the Greek" (ESV). But here he writes about the Jew and Greek in reverse order. He first concentrates on the problem of the Gentile.

To be sure, neither the word *Greek* nor the word *Gentile* is found in these verses, but Paul obviously has the non-Jew in mind. His descriptions of idolatry (1:23) and immoral behavior (1:26–27) are apt depictions of first-century pagan culture.

Yet Paul is not exclusively addressing the Gentiles' situation. His words bear a striking similarity to Old Testament passages (see Psalm 106:20; Jeremiah 2:11) that describe Israel's sin in worshipping the golden calf and other false gods. So even though his attention here seems to be directed toward the Gentile, his point is the basic sinfulness of all people, Jew and Gentile alike.

Throughout Romans, Paul engages in dialectical arguments, in which he anticipates and articulates the responses of someone expressing the opposing viewpoint. In this passage, some biblical scholars believe that Paul is doing the same thing: presenting a rhetorical argument, articulating the prevailing view of the Jews toward Gentiles in his day. Though the chapter ends with verse 32, there is no break in the arguments being expressed. Pointing to Romans 2:1, these Bible scholars suggest that Paul's words in verses 18–32 are neither his own thoughts nor those of God, per se, but rather they echo the arguments made by the Jewish people to distinguish and separate themselves from the pagans by giving a laundry list of behaviors that Jewish people prided themselves in avoiding. Other biblical experts interpret it straightforwardly, that Paul was passing on his God-inspired thoughts in his letter to the Romans.

God's Wrath

For many people, the concept of the wrath of God (1:18) seems to contradict the idea of a God of love. How could the God who loved the world so much that He gave His Son (John 3:16) also turn His wrath toward sinful humanity? Is this a contradiction in the New Testament picture of God? No, not for Paul. For him, the wrath of God is not opposed to the love of God. The two realities are like two sides of the same coin. Both are revealed in the gospel (1:17–18).

Our confusion may well lie in thinking that God's wrath is similar to human anger. The human emotion of anger is often inconsistent, irrational, and capricious. Suppose, for example, that you have had a particularly rough day at work, traffic is unusually heavy on the way home, and you get a flat tire on the freeway. When you finally get home, your first reaction is to "jump down the throat" of the first person you see—even a loved one who is not responsible for the unfortunate set of circumstances you have experienced. Your temper flares and you turn your anger toward an innocent person. Knowing how we humans handle anger, we shudder to think of God as capable of the same kind of wrath. And He isn't.

For Paul, human anger and divine wrath are not the same kind of emotional reaction. Because of our imperfection and humanness, our anger erupts on a whim. God's wrath, however, is the response of One who is totally good and totally loving. It is a response that recoils from anything that defiles, distorts, or corrupts the goodness God intended for His created order. It is a rejection of the evil that exists in our world.

How then is God's wrath revealed in the gospel? In the same way that His righteousness is revealed. We discover or experience both based on our response to God's offer of grace. Just as righteousness becomes a reality for a person if he or she chooses to accept it, so the wrath of God is experienced by a person who chooses to reject Him. To decide against one is to decide for the other.

The Cause of God's Wrath

God's wrath is His reaction to ungodliness and unrighteousness (1:18), but in the case of the Gentile—the non-Jew—is this a fair response? Since the Gentiles had not known God through God's self-disclosure to Israel, how could they be held accountable?

That is an important question, and Paul answers it by telling us that every person in all time has received a revelation from God in creation (1:20). Throughout the Bible the idea of God's revelation is always to be understood in terms of His self-disclosure. What God reveals is Himself. In the created order the invisible One is actually seen (1:20) by the eyes of faith. As the Psalmist said, "The heavens declare the glory of God, and the sky above proclaims his handiwork" (Psalm 19:1, ESV).

But not everyone has seen or recognized God's revelation of Himself in creation. That is true, of course, but the problem isn't with the revelation but with the person who refuses to see what has been revealed. For example, you are listening to the radio, and the station broadcasts an emergency alert just after you turn the radio off. The radio station is still broadcasting at full strength, but your radio is not receiving its transmission. Simply because God has not been recognized and worshipped does not mean His revelation of Himself is inadequate. The failure belongs to the one who rejects or ignores the revelation. As the old adage goes, "There's none so blind as those who will not see." And so, by refusing to respond to God, by closing their eyes to the light of the gospel, the Gentiles' "foolish hearts were darkened" (1:21, NIV).

Because of this willful blindness, the Gentile "exchanged the glory of the immortal God for images made to look like a mortal human being and birds and animals and reptiles" (1:23, NIV; see also verse 25). For this reason, then, the nonbeliever has become subject to God's wrath. For the person who responds positively to the revelation of God, the result is relationship with God. But for the one who rejects His revelation, the result is God's wrath.

The Consequences of God's Wrath

We come next to an important question: What are the consequences of God's wrath? How is it experienced? (1:24–32). For many people, the concept of wrath always conveys the idea of direct divine punishment. It certainly did for Jonathan Edwards, the noted Puritan preacher. In his famous sermon "Sinners in the Hands of an Angry God," he pictured God as One who dangles sinners over the pit of hell.

For Paul, however, God's wrath has been experienced by people in another way. The results of the divine wrath are realized in this lifetime by the person who rejects God's revelation: "God gave them up" (1:24, ESV) or "God gave them over" (NIV). Notice the wording. Paul does not say that God gives up *on* humankind; rather He gives humankind up, so that they suffer the consequences of their own actions. After all, aren't the most effective disciplinary acts that we parents impose on our children those in which they are forced to suffer the consequences of what they have done? The old saying applies: "You've made your bed; now lie in it." According to Paul, this is in effect what God is saying to sinful humanity. God has created us to be truly free, but the freedom to choose is meaningless if choice is not followed by consequences.

Three times in these verses Paul said, "God also gave them up"; "God gave them up"; "God gave them over" (1:24, 26, 28, KJV) to their own sinful ways. The results of this action are twofold.

First, one's personhood is affected. Paul gives as an example "sexual impurity for the degrading of their bodies with one another" (1:24, NIV), which is followed immediately by the statement that they "exchanged the truth about God for a lie, and worshipped and served created things rather than the Creator" (1:25, NIV), keeping these statements within Paul's larger argument about the practice of paganism and idolatry (see also verse 23) by Gentile unbelievers in God.

Second, relationships with other people are damaged. When a person rejects God and chooses not to take Him as Savior and Lord, he or she takes on a Godless behavior. Paul lists a whole catalog of vices that wreak havoc in relationships and ultimately alienate one person from another (1:28–32). We won't list them all here, but as you reread these verses, you will see that these sins run from disobedience to parents, to backbiting, envy, deceit, and murder.

Particularly intriguing is the statement in verse 28b in which it is implied that not only are such people involved in committing these sins, but also they affirm and approve of others who commit them. In other words, not only are these actions despicable, but so are those who, though technically innocent of committing the acts themselves, stand by and watch with approval others who do them.

Paul's picture of the unbelieving Gentile is of one in a dire predicament. Refusing to acknowledge the self-disclosing God, fooling himself into thinking that he is wise, he worships the creature rather than the Creator. And he pays the consequences. Creature worship—the worship of things, substitutes for God—exacts a heavy price even today.

The Failings of the Jews (2:1–3:8)
In the last part of our lesson we saw that Paul concentrated on the predicament of the Gentile without ever using the specific

term *Gentile* or *Greek*. A similar situation is found in these verses in that he seems to be concentrating his attention on the Jews, although the word *Jew* is not mentioned until he writes, ". . . you call yourself a Jew . . ." (2:17, NIV).

It is true that Paul addresses one whom he calls "a foolish person" (NASB) in verses 1–16 and that he then addresses the Jews in the next verse. However, between verse 16 and verse 17 there does not seem to be an abrupt change of subject. Paul continues to talk to the same person. Furthermore, as we shall see, the criticisms that Paul offers to this person in the first sixteen verses are particularly applicable to the Jews as well. However, as in the last section, once again Paul's comments are not limited to the Jews. Remember that in this portion of his letter he is writing about the universal sinfulness of humankind.

One other feature of this part of our lesson should be noted. Paul is using a particular writing style technically known as a *dialectic*. This term simply indicates that the author develops his line of thought by carrying on a conversation or debate with an imaginary opponent. It will help us to understand these verses and others that follow in the letter when we see that some statements are made by Paul to express the sentiment of this imaginary opponent. Such statements are made (sometimes in the form of a question) so that Paul can respond with his own view.

The Jew and God's Judgment

In the Old Testament, the people of Israel had been called to be the special people of God. This calling was not just to a privileged status but also to a purpose: They were to be a light to the nations, to attract all people—even Gentiles—to the worship of God. Israel, though, had failed miserably. Instead of reaching out and attracting others, they had withdrawn into themselves. They were content to rest on the laurels of privilege and to forget about responsibility (2:1–11).

Moreover, the Jews in Paul's day had a reputation of being somewhat smug about their status with God. They felt they were superior to everyone else and in a position to judge others. In *The Wisdom of Solomon*, a popular piece of Jewish literature from the first century BC, the Jews were actually accused of having such a false pride. This unfounded feeling of superiority had led them to believe that they would be less severely punished than Gentiles for committing the same sins.

Evidently this harsh, judgmental attitude is in Paul's mind as he begins to describe the failings of the Jews. Notice the play on words in these eleven verses. At least seven times Paul uses the terms *judge* or *judgment*. The Jew who is quick to judge will himself be judged. Reminiscent of the Sermon on the Mount (see especially Matthew 7:1–5), Paul's words here remind his readers that the person who judges someone else is subject to judgment. *Whenever we judge another, we invite others to judge us.*

A further problem for Paul, though, is that the Jews were quick to judge others for the same acts they were guilty of (2:1–3). This seems to be a universal human trait. We tend to feel that the only way to improve our self-esteem is by putting everyone else down. Paul makes it clear here that the "mere human being" (verse 3, NIV) or "foolish person" (NASB) to whom he is speaking believes that the quickest way to succeed is to devalue the worth of another person. By making someone else look worse, he thinks he makes himself look better. Ironically, the things he condemns others for doing are the very actions that he himself has done.

This was the sin that God confronted Adam with in the garden. Had he and Eve not disobeyed the same commandment? But Adam tried to make himself look better in God's eyes by placing the blame on Eve. According to Adam's own reasoning, he was not nearly as guilty as Eve, for she had "made" him eat the forbidden fruit (see Genesis 3). As sons and daughters of Adam, we see ourselves committing this sin.

Paul criticized the Jews for the same kind of behavior. Thinking that they are more precious in God's eyes, they presumed upon God's kindness (2:4) and assumed that they would not be judged for the same sins he condemns others of. Paul insists, though, that those who think that way are actually storing up God's wrath for themselves, and that they, too, will face God's judgment (2:5).

As a matter of fact, everyone—Jew and Greek (Gentile) alike—will be judged according to their actions (2:6–10). What a sobering thought! We will be held accountable, not so much for what we believe but for what we put into practice— the way we act. It's not unusual to hear from Christian pulpits that we must "believe" the right things. Usually this means that we are to agree with the particular creed or confession of the one writing or preaching. But throughout the Bible, Old Testament as well as New, we are reminded again and again that we will be judged for the things we *do*. This is such an important point that you might want to stop a few moments and read the following scripture references: Psalm 62:12, Proverbs 24:12, and Jeremiah 17:10 from the Old Testament; Matthew 7:21 and 16:27 from the teachings of Jesus. It is our actions, not our profession, that count!

Do you remember the letter to the church at Ephesus that is recorded in the book of Revelation (verse 2:1 and following)? That church was commended by Christ for *believing* the right things, but it was condemned for its failure to *do* the right thing: to love. The Christian life must never be reduced to a list of things that we are to believe; it must always include the idea that those beliefs are to be put into practice. As James 2:18 tells us, "But someone will say, 'You have faith and I have works.' Show me your faith apart from your works, and I will show you my faith by my works" (ESV). Belief and behavior are inseparable!

But not only does God judge based on our actions, Paul insists that He judges impartially. The Jew cannot presume upon his election by God; he is not given a superior standing nor a privileged status that exempts him from God's judgment. The Jew, like the Greek (Gentile), has sinned in God's eyes. Both have failed. Both need a new and right relationship with God. And, as we will see in the next lesson, God has provided for both in the same way—through faith, for "God does not show favoritism" (2:11, NIV).

The Jews and God's Law
But what about the Law? Had not the Jews been a recipient of this special revelation from God? Did this not give them special status and therefore exemption from judgment?

In these verses, Paul clarifies this relationship (2:12–24). There is a distinction to be made between Jew and Gentile, based not on inherited differences but on revelation, on God's disclosure of Himself. But the distinction does not provide for partiality in judgment.

The Law does give a different basis for judgment. *Everyone* who sins under the Law will be judged on the basis of the Law, and, by implication, the one who sins without a knowledge of the Law will be judged accordingly (2:12). Each person is judged on the basis of how God has made Himself known to him or her. For the Jew, that revelation is synonymous with the Law. For the Gentile, God has revealed Himself in creation (see 1:19–20).

Yet another source of revelation is the *conscience* (2:15). Certainly conscience does not provide the same quality of revelation as that which has come through the Law, but conscience can lead one to right action. It is at this point, though, that the Jew receives a sharp condemnation because while he has had the more perfect revelation of God through the Law, he has failed to live up to its standards. But at times the Gentile, even though he has not known the Law, has fulfilled its requirements by following the dictates of his conscience (2:14–15). However, the one who finds favor in God's judgment is not the person who *hears* the requirements of the Law (the Jew) but the one who *does* what the Law demands. "For it is not those who *hear* the law who are righteous in God's sight, but it is those who *obey* the law who will be declared righteous" (2:13, NIV; italics added for emphasis). James picks up on this same idea: "Do not merely listen to the word, and so deceive yourselves. Do what it says" (James 1:22, NIV).

When a Jewish believer speaks about knowledge of God and of relationship with Him and then breaks the Law he claims to uphold, he drives others away from God rather than bringing them to Him (2:17–24). Here is the age-old problem of people not practicing what they preach.

Paul indicates that this is the problem of the Jewish people. They were called to be a "light" to the nations, to attract all people to the worship of God. He proclaims the Law as the superior revelation of God. But by his failure to uphold that Law, he repels the Gentiles whom he has been called to attract. And to further emphasize his point, Paul quotes Isaiah 52:5: "The name of God is blasphemed among the Gentiles because of you" (2:24, ESV).

The True Jew

To Paul's line of reasoning that these Jewish believers have also failed in God's eyes, a Jewish believer might argue that circumcision is an indication of his special relationship with God that sets him apart from the Gentile (2:25–29). This ancient rite, dating back to Abraham (Genesis 17:10 and following), was a visible sign that the Jew was a member of the covenant community; that he, too, was an heir to the promises of God. To the Jewish person of the day, the performance of this rite was so important that it even took precedence over Sabbath regulations. It was to be performed on that day despite the Law's injunctions about Sabbath rest. It was the most important religious rite in Judaism. It was so identified with the covenant relationship that some rabbis insisted that a Jew could not be condemned to Gehenna (hell) without the removal of the mark of circumcision.

It is very easy for us to be critical of the Jews to whom Paul was speaking, but many modern so-called Christians are not without fault at this point. Even though they don't live up to the ethical and spiritual standards of Christianity, they delude themselves into believing they are right with God because they were raised in a Christian home, they have been baptized, or their name is on a church roll somewhere. They feel they have a guaranteed relationship with God.

For Paul, though, such an outward sign is useless unless it is accompanied by appropriate behavior (2:25). The uncircumcised person who keeps the Law has better standing with God than the circumcised man who violates it (2:26–27).

Relationship with God is not based on anything that is outward, external, or physical (2:28). And the term *Jew* as Paul uses it in verses 28–29 does not simply mean a person of a particular ethnicity. A true Jew, then, is not one who has a certain family tree or has submitted to a particular religious rite. The true Jew is one who is so inwardly, just as true circumcision is not an outward physical rite but an inner attitude of the heart (2:29). The kind of person Paul is talking about in these verses is one who is rightly related to God.

The Advantage of the Jew

From the line of argument so far in our lesson, in which Paul continues his discussion or debate with his imaginary opponent, we might conclude that for Paul there was then no advantage in being a Jew. But he could never agree with that proposition (3:1–8). In fact, in verse 2 he says there is a great advantage, "much in every way!" (NIV). Although he will return to this theme later and mention other advantages (see 9:4–5), he specifically points out here that the Jew has received the oracles—the revelation of God, God's self-disclosure, in the Law. The Jew has been privileged, but the privilege carries the responsibility of obedience. The disobedience of the Jew does not minimize the advantage; neither does it indicate a failure on the part of God. Rather, the faithlessness of the Jew has simply caused the faithfulness of God to stand out even more. Paul further supports his position by quoting (3:4) from the Old Testament (Psalm 51:4). Here the imagery is of a court of law where God and humankind contend with each other, but from which God emerges as vindicated, as right.

With lawyerlike precision, Paul then takes the next step in his argument: If the unrighteousness of humankind simply makes God's righteousness more prominent, is God then unfair to subject mankind to His wrath? Paul responds with a resounding *no*! "God forbid" (3:6, KJV). And Paul now sums up this part of his argument by saying that the Jew who has benefitted from God's special disclosure of Himself but who has failed to live by the Law is justly condemned (3:8). Like the Gentile, the Jew, too, has failed before God.

The Universal Sinfulness of Humankind (3:9–20)

In these verses Paul concludes that the failure of humankind is universal. Jew and Gentile alike have been overpowered by sin. "All, both Jews and Greeks, are under sin" (3:9, ESV). The failure of both Jew and Gentile can be summed up in this one word—*sin*. Even though the plural form—*sins*—is frequently used in the rest of the New Testament, Paul doesn't use that form here. He doesn't seem to think of humankind's predicament in terms of individual sins. Instead, sin seems to be seen as an overwhelming force that has engulfed the human race.

Paul then connects his argument here to a collection of references from the Old Testament that suggests virtually every aspect of humankind has been dominated by sin (3:10–18). Take just a moment and compare these verses with Psalms 5:9, 10:7, 14:1–2, 26:1, 53:1–2, and 140:3; and Isaiah 59:7–8. These verses confirm that every part of the human race is under the dominion of sin.

Paul now closes his discussion and our lesson by insisting that the Law—probably meant here to mean the entire Old Testament—does not provide the answer for humankind's sin dilemma. Instead, it only makes humankind aware of sin (3:19–20). A vivid picture from a court of law is used in the phrase "that every mouth may be silenced" (verse 19, NIV). The figure suggested is that of a defendant in a trial who has been confronted with such overwhelming evidence against him that there is nothing he can say in his own defense—he is speechless!

While Paul's arguments and writing in this lesson may at times seem a bit belabored and technical to our modern ears, we, like his first readers, need to walk through them with him. In these complex days of the twenty-first century, we live in a world racked by violence and threats of terrorism and war. So many people have refused to recognize a God revealed in His creation and in conscience or the Law. We have been guilty of building ourselves up at the expense of others and have accused others publicly of the same sins we've committed privately.

As we look around us, as we read the headlines and news websites and listen to the television or radio newscasts with their stories of child abuse, political polarization, murder, family infighting and collapse, and despots bent on expansionism or destruction, we have to admit that Paul was right. We're all in the same boat. All have sinned and are candidates for God's remedy—salvation through Jesus Christ.

◆————————————————————◆

Father God, thank You for Your salvation and the opportunity to learn more about You and Your Word. AMEN.

What if some were unfaithful? Will their unfaithfulness nullify God's faithfulness? Not at all! . . . This righteousness is given through faith in Jesus Christ to all who believe.

—Romans 3:3–4, 22, NIV

A few years ago I was flipping through my journal pages, beginning with January of the new year. That last year had been a particularly trying time, and it seemed like my eyes focused only on myself. My personal needs and problems jumped off the page, not to mention my failures.

Sometimes the refusal to let "memories be forgotten" and the harsh focus on our own faithlessness cause us to forget the meaning of grace, and what Jesus has done in our lives.

Fortunately, in the middle of my memory journey, Jesus reminded me of His love for me, faults and all. So I started reading through the pages again. This time I saw answers to prayer, victories won, and praises recorded again and again: times of grace, mercy, and Jesus's faithfulness.

As believers, our faithlessness or self-criticism, be it true, false, or exaggerated, never cancels out Jesus's faithfulness. His forgiveness and grace always rise higher. We will fail often. But Jesus never intended for us to focus on our human weakness. He made a way. We don't have to earn enough good points to negate the bad. He set things right between us and God.

He faithfully carried out God's plan and died for us despite our faithlessness. At the start of each new year and all year long, Jesus makes all things new.

—*Rebecca Barlow Jordan*

Notes

Notes

Notes

The Provision of God: Salvation through Justification by Faith

Lord God, thank You for Your love, which shows itself even in Your provisions for me. AMEN.

A gifted college history professor was adept at stimulating her students' interest in her subject. Her lectures were masterpieces—not only in content but also in timing. Frequently, in reconstructing events from the past, she would pace her lecture in such a way that at the end of the class period, the central character was left in some dire predicament from which there seemed to be no escape—a cliffhanger. When the class bell rang, the students were on the edges of their seats, wondering what was going to happen. Many times they were left so enthralled that they couldn't wait until the next class period. They actually rushed to their books to read for themselves the outcome of the incident!

You could say that Paul left readers with a cliffhanger in Romans 3. After talking at length about the plight of the human race in 1:18–3:8, Paul concluded his discussion in verses 9–20 by reiterating the dire state of humankind. Without exception, everyone—whether Jew or Greek—has sinned. Everyone has failed to live responsibly with and responsively to the dramatic disclosure that has been received from God.

Confronted with such grim reality, a reader of these verses, like the history student, is left on the edge of his or her seat, wondering if there is any hope, any escape, any solution to the problem the human race has created for itself. Then suddenly in verse 21, we are confronted with the opening of the next episode as Paul makes a dramatic shift in the discussion. "But now the righteousness of God has been manifested apart from the law" (ESV). The sin predicament of mankind is resolved by God's provision! Our salvation is provided for; we are justified—made righteous—by faith.

The Means of Justification: God's Activity in Jesus Christ (3:21–31)

The words *but now* are used rhetorically to connect what Paul wishes to describe here with what he has just discussed, but the connection is made as a contrast. What he now describes is vastly different from the plight depicted in the preceding verses. But the words are not simply a literary device to contrast two thoughts. The word *now* also has a literal, temporal sense. Something has happened in the recent past that makes a difference in the present. God has done something in Jesus Christ.

In earlier times the righteousness of God had been revealed through the Law. But that revelation, though intended for good, had not fully achieved its desired effect. Humankind had fallen away from God despite it. Now, however, God's righteousness, His activity of making us right, has been manifested apart from the Law. Yet, ironically, as Paul will demonstrate with selections from the scriptures, this righteousness is attested to in the Old Testament, ". . . although the Law and the Prophets bear witness to it" (3:21, ESV).

And this righteousness is made available through faith—belief in Jesus Christ. The words in the King James Version, ". . . by faith *of* Jesus Christ . . ." (3:22; italics added for emphasis), do not mean the faith belonging to Jesus Christ but our faith in Him, as they are translated in more recent versions: "through faith *in* Jesus Christ" (NIV; italics added for emphasis). We should never forget that faith in this sense means trust and commitment and openness to God in Christ. Faith does not mean believing in a list of statements *about* Christ. It means believing *in* Him. He, not doctrines about Him, is the object of faith.

Here then is Paul's understanding of the solution to the sin problem of the human race. Universal sinfulness is challenged by the universal possibility of salvation.

Just as all have sinned (3:23), salvation is available for all who will believe (3:22). To grapple with the meaning of salvation, Paul uses in the next few verses three different metaphors drawn from three aspects of first-century life that paint word pictures of what God has done in Christ.

Pictures are important for learning and understanding. The very first books that children "read" are picture books. Pictures can tell stories. We treasure snapshots and photographs because of the events they call to mind. Pictures or illustrations are indispensable as we try to assemble products that we have purchased. And when we try to explain an idea to someone else, don't we frequently resort to drawing a picture, no matter how limited our artistic abilities may be?

Paul knew the value of pictures. Though he did not draw them with a pen, he painted them with his words. When he had a concept that was unfamiliar to his readers, he explained his idea with one or more word pictures that would conjure up an image in his readers' minds. Sometimes we miss the significance of this picture language because the words do not project for us the same images they did for those who first read them. Then, too, we have frequently missed the picture because the words have become so worn or so familiar that they fail to stimulate our imaginations. That's the way it is with the words Paul has used here to picture the meaning of salvation. Let's try to look at them as if we hadn't seen them before, just as Paul's first readers would have done.

Justification

The first of the pictures (3:24–26) that Paul suggests is taken from the court of law, the idea of "justification" that we have already discussed in lesson 1. Especially for Jewish Christian readers, this concept provided an apt description of God's activity in Christ. After centuries of living by the Law, these people would understand this metaphor drawn from legal terminology.

They could easily understand their plight in terms of law breaking, the failure to comply with all the requirements of the Law. Furthermore, justification—God's act of making them right despite their failures—spoke to them of God's grace.

It is important for us to remember that Paul was a Jewish Christian. As we shall see in our study of Romans 7, he had known the privilege of being entrusted with the Law, God's disclosure of Himself.

But he had also known the frustration of not being able to live up to the expectations of the Law. As interpreted by the Pharisees, the party of which Paul was a member, the Law had become a complex structure in the first century.

Not only did the concept of Law include the written regulations in the Old Testament, but it also included the oral interpretations and proscriptions of that written Law that were handed down from rabbi to rabbi. In reference to the proper observance of the Sabbath, for example, there were approximately 1,500 rules that were included in this oral material. So many rules or laws existed that the ordinary person felt a sense of futility regarding the Law. It was virtually impossible to *know* all of it, much less *keep* it. Paul knew this feeling of inadequacy with regard to the Law; perhaps that is why he seized upon the idea of justification as an appropriate picture of God's provision for overcoming the plight of humankind.

Justification might not strike us with the same impact as it did for Paul's first readers. Most of us don't necessarily see ourselves as lawbreakers. In fact, in some people's way of thinking, American law and the Christian faith are so entwined that we delude ourselves about our relationship with God. We think because we are law-abiding citizens that we are automatically in good stead with God. We tend to follow this kind of reasoning: "I obey the law; therefore I am a *just* person. Since I am just, then by definition I must also be *right* with God." But a person can be a good citizen and fail to be rightly related to God. After all, living in America does not make one a Christian.

Using a very contemporary illustration may help us to come to a better understanding of what Paul wants us to see in his teaching on justification. Word-processing programs have the capability to "justify" margins. With a couple of keystrokes or the press of a mouse button, this feature allows the writer or editor to command the machine to make every typed line the same length.

Do you remember our first look at the word *justification* in the first lesson? We saw there that it means more than just calling someone right who is not; it has the idea of actually making that person right. That meaning is obvious in the use of the term in reference to margins on a typed page. A word-processing program does not just look at an irregular margin and *call* it right (justified); it actually makes it right.

In this picture of what God has done in Christ, Paul also has this meaning in mind. Justification is not just calling the sinner right. It is not even simply acquitting the guilty. Justification is God's act of making one right once again! God demonstrates His righteousness by His righteous activity. He shows that he is just by justifying (making righteous) the sinner (3:26).

As we have seen before, however, in these verses, Paul associates this idea with two other key concepts: grace (3:24) and faith (3:26). Not only does justification show God's righteousness, but it also demonstrates His grace. Justification comes to us as a gift. We have not earned or merited God's favor. Salvation is freely bestowed upon us through our belief.

Paul stresses again in these verses that humankind is universally sinful: "For all have sinned, and come short of the glory of God" (3:23, KJV). He does not, however, suggest that humankind is universally saved in Jesus Christ. The possibility of universal salvation Paul would not deny; Christ's death was "potentially" effective for everyone. Practically, though, salvation is limited to those who believe.

Redemption

Paul next gives us a second picture. The setting here is a slave market (3:24). In the first century, slavery was a part of everyday life. Although the Roman government had not created this system of servitude, it certainly had promoted it and profited from it. The Roman Empire had practically conquered the known world, and with that conquest had come an enhancement of the role of slavery in society. Captured peoples were brought to Rome to be paraded before cheering spectators as living spoils of battle. They were then coerced into a life of bondage, serving as laborers in the fields, as domestic servants in the villas of the wealthy, as clerical and governmental workers, as the chief source of labor for commerce and industry. Although no precise figures can be known with certainty, estimates of the number of enslaved people in the Roman Empire have run as high as 60 percent of the population.

Integral to the system of slavery was the slave market. Here the captives and those born into slavery were bought and sold. Every once in a while, some fortunate enslaved people had their purchase price paid by a benefactor who then gave them their freedom. The word for this transaction was "redemption."

Again this term has lost some of its significance for us today. Even though "redemption" is a word we hear in church, for most of us its meaning as Paul used it is not especially clear to us now. Redemption is something we do now with rewards points for either merchandise or cash. It is no wonder then that when we tell people today they need to be "redeemed," it may well produce nothing more than confusion. After all, they see no similarity between themselves and rewards points!

But in Paul's day, this metaphor made a profound impact. His first-century readers knew both the dread of slavery and the desirability of deliverance. They could well understand the significance of the atonement of Christ in terms of paying the purchase price for the emancipation of the enslaved person.

Propitiation

Like justification and redemption, Paul's third picture dealing with salvation is somewhat strange to the modern reader (3:25–26). "Propitiation" is a metaphor that is drawn from the system of worship in which animals were sacrificed.

Modern understanding of this term is further complicated by several factors. First, it is a word that we encounter rarely, if ever, in our everyday reading. Second, different English versions of the New Testament do not agree about the proper translation of the original Greek term that Paul wrote. While the King James Version and most modern translations use "propitiation," a few modern translations, such as the Revised Standard Version, employ the term "expiation."

Propitiation and expiation do not mean the same thing. Propitiation is synonymous with appeasement, and it is a somewhat passive idea as far as God is concerned, for God is the object of the action implied. According to this idea, a person does something to appease an angry God. A price is paid to remove God's displeasure.

Expiation, on the other hand, is defined as "the act of making amends for" something, or "to extinguish the guilt incurred by" a person. Expiation indicates an activity of God. He is not the passive recipient of the action but the One who does the acting. Sin is the object of the verb. Sin is expiated; it is covered, blotted out, or obliterated—extinguished. This action only God can do.

Which term then best translates the idea that Paul had in mind? In Christ's crucifixion, did Paul see God being placated (propitiation) or God wiping sin away (expiation)?

All of this probably seems a bit complicated, but it has been said that Romans 3:25–26 contains more gospel than any other two verses in the Bible. Such being the case, it is important that we have as clear a picture as possible of what Paul really meant.

Bible scholars, and clearly also Bible translators, differ about which one is the better, more accurate word to communicate the meaning. If we study the same two words in the Hebrew of the Old Testament and then examine carefully the use of these words in first-century Greek, we might well conclude that the word *expiation* is to be preferred in 3:25. According to this idea, God sent His Son to our world as a means of obliterating sin, not of placating Himself.

One other alternative translation for this term is possible. Again drawing from the imagery of sacrifice, one could perhaps express the idea as "mercy seat." The mercy seat was the cover over the Ark of the Covenant in the Holy of Holies in the tabernacle and the temple. It was here that the high priest sprinkled the blood of the sacrifice as an act of atonement. It was here that God met the Jewish worshipper, and it was here that sin was forgiven.

If "mercy seat" is Paul's idea here in this verse, he then means that in the experience of Christ Jesus on the Cross, God provided a new mercy seat. Just as blood was sprinkled on the old mercy seat as an atoning act, so "God presented Christ as a sacrifice of atonement" (3:25, NIV). Jesus is the new "place" where God meets us and where our sins are forgiven.

Again, Paul's metaphor, though meaningful to his first-century readers, is somewhat removed from us. The picture has to be explained. As we will see in our next lesson, when we study Romans 5, Paul has yet another word to describe salvation, one that more vividly speaks to us: "reconciliation."

Paul uses many metaphors—language pictures—to describe God's solution to the plight of humankind. *Justification, redemption, expiation,* and *reconciliation* are different ways of picturing the same reality, but not one of them by itself completely does the job. Salvation is a greater reality than any one word can convey.

The Role of Faith

In verse 25 Paul mentioned faith as the key to our receiving this gift of salvation that God has freely offered. Now, in verses 27–31, he reaffirms its importance. As you reread these five verses, you will discover that since our salvation becomes real through faith, we have no basis for being boastful. Paul then goes on to make it clear that we are not rightly related to God because of our works (3:27) or our adherence to the Law (3:28) or our ancestry (3:29). We are saved through faith—the openness to God that allows us to accept what God offers.

The Meaning of Faith: The Example of Abraham (4:1–25)

Perhaps anticipating the reaction of some of his readers to his explanation of faith-righteousness, Paul reverts to his use of dialectic once again. In this debate with an imaginary opponent, he voices both the anticipated objections of his readers and his responses to them.

What arguments might his opponents offer to counter his understanding of justification by faith alone? Those with a Jewish background might take exception to what he has said about the importance of faith by recalling the experience of the patriarch Abraham, the founder of the Jewish nation. Scripture (Genesis 15:6) indicates that Abraham had been justified, made righteous, by God. But in the rabbinic tradition, he had been granted this status on the basis of the works that he had done. They believe his circumcision was proof of this. Moreover, though Abraham had lived before Moses and the giving of the Law, the Jewish teachers speculated that his righteousness was an indication that he had anticipated the Law and that he had actually observed it in advance.

Furthermore, the Jews assumed that they, too, could have a right relationship with God if they observed the same legal and ritual requirements. Ironically, though, they also felt that they had a head start on achieving righteousness simply on the basis of their physical descent from Abraham. They had inherited an advantage with God on the basis of what their ancestor had accomplished!

To illustrate his understanding of faith, then, Paul could have no better model than Abraham. This ancient patriarch "proved" for the Jews their understanding of justification based on works. Paul, though, will use illustrations from Abraham's life to indicate just the opposite. Jewish detractors thought Abraham was the supreme example of a person being made righteous by works. By showing that even he was saved by faith, not by works, Paul will demonstrate that faith alone provides the possibility for right standing before God.

Abraham and Works

Paul opens this discussion (4:1–8) by stating the argument of his imaginary opponent: "What then shall we say that Abraham, our forefather according to the flesh, has found?" (4:1, NASB). Although some of the modern translations use a Greek text that does not include the word for "find," the idea is a common expression from the Greek version of the Old Testament that refers to the finding of grace or mercy. For those who could claim Abraham as a physical ancestor, there was the understanding that he had "found" mercy on the basis of his works. In fact, literature from the intertestamental period insisted that Abraham was perfect in all of his deeds.

But Paul contradicts this idea. If, after all, Abraham had been justified on the basis of the things he had done, he would have had some grounds for boasting about his accomplishments (4:2). But the Old Testament story does not show Abraham as one who took pride in his own actions. Rather, he simply believed God—had faith in Him—and on this basis, he was accepted by God as being righteous. "Abraham believed God, and it was credited to him as righteousness" (4:3, NIV, quoting Genesis 15:6).

Again, according to some rabbinic teaching, Abraham's faith was in itself a work or an action that gained God's favor; by believing in God, Abraham "earned" salvation. That this was not the case is indicated in verses 4 and 5. If Abraham had earned his position before God, his righteousness would have been due him, just as wages are owed to a laborer for the work he has accomplished (4:4). Abraham's faith, though, was an openness to receive what God freely offered. The righteousness he received was not a wage that had been earned; it was a gift (grace) that had been bestowed upon him.

According to Paul, Abraham's righteousness was not something he had earned. He had not merited God's favor. He was not given a reward for something he had done. Rather, God had bestowed His grace upon Abraham; He had freely given it to Abraham by His own choice. Abraham's faith was not a work that forced a bargain from God. It was an openness to God, a responsiveness by which he accepted what God had given him.

Abraham, too, was a sinner; he was ungodly. But he trusted in the God who had justified him, who had put him in right standing (4:5). Again we must remember the basic meaning of justification. It is not simply the acquittal of the guilty; it is not merely calling one right who is not. It is actually "making" him right.

Certainly a person who is justified apart from works is truly blessed, truly happy. This understanding is affirmed for Paul in Psalm 32:1–2, which he quotes in verses 7–8. As a matter of fact, Paul apparently links these verses with Genesis 15:6 on the basis of the word *impute* (KJV), which is found in both. Since the word is not particularly familiar to our everyday speech, modern translations use other words to express its meaning: "credits" (NASB, NIV) or "counts" (ESV). It means "to ascribe to another." As the New International Version translates it: "Blessed is the one whose sin the Lord will never count against them." For Paul, then, imputing (counting or crediting) righteousness is the same reality as not imputing (counting) sin.

Abraham and Circumcision

Paul now turns to a discussion of circumcision, one of the foremost distinctions of Judaism, and relates it to Abraham (4:9–12). Dating back to Abraham, this rite provided a physical mark that identified a man as being a member of the covenant community of God.

Circumcision was a "work," a deed that was performed. First-century Jews were confident that because they had done this ritual act, they had *earned* a relationship with God. In looking back at Abraham, they felt that his circumcision was a work that had guaranteed his standing with God.

Referring back to Psalm 32:1–2, Paul then questions his imaginary opponent: Is this blessed state bestowed upon one who is uncircumcised, or is it reserved for the circumcised only (4:9)? In the case of Abraham, this blessedness—being made righteous—was bestowed "before" he was circumcised, not after (4:10). In fact, it was 14 years before. Genesis 15:6 recalls the experience of Abraham before the birth of Ishmael, who was born when his father was 86 years old (Genesis 16:16). Abraham was not circumcised until he was 99 (Genesis 17:1 and following)!

Circumcision, then, did not earn God's favor for Abraham. Rather, it was seen as a sign or an authentication of the righteousness that he received by faith when he was still uncircumcised (4:11). Faith, not circumcision, is the key to one's relationship with God. Consequently, Abraham is the father of all who have faith, whether they are circumcised or not (4:11–12).

For us, it may seem like Paul was belaboring a point, but especially for his Jewish readers his emphasis was urgently needed. The lesson for us here is that religious ritual does not enable a person to be saved. We are saved by faith. The ritual is the sign or the pointer to the reality that salvation has taken place.

Abraham and the Law

What about the Law, specifically the Mosaic Code? Paul's Jewish contemporaries were confident that their keeping of the Law was their assurance of participation in the covenant relationship with God. Because of the supreme worth that they placed on the Law, they exercised some mental gymnastics and concluded that Abraham must have observed all of the Law *even before it was given.*

Paul, however, interprets the Old Testament story chronologically (4:13–15). Abraham was called righteous generations before the giving of the Law at Sinai. His act of faith preceded the giving of the Law by more than 400 years! The promises that God gave to Abraham were most certainly not conditioned upon his observance of a law code that would not be known for centuries. Instead, Abraham received God's promises through faith-righteousness. In fact, Paul says that if only those who obey the Law are heirs to God's promises, then both faith and the promises are null and void (4:13–14). And then if we take the argument to its logical conclusion, we would have to say that if relationship with God is based on rigid adherence to the Law of Moses, the previous relationship of Abraham with God is invalidated.

In verse 15 Paul is not suggesting that there is no sin apart from the Law. The tendency to sin is present even in the absence of the Law. But technically, Paul believed there is no violation of the Law until there is a Law. For example, many years ago, the highway speed limit in most states was 75 miles per hour. In the 1970s the United States' oil supplies were severely curtailed by the OPEC oil embargo. So, in an initiative to curb America's oil consumption, a new law took effect that limited the maximum speed to 55. Those who had driven 75 miles per hour under the old speed limit were not tried or fined as lawbreakers after the new law took effect. They had not broken the law at that time because the law did not exist at that time.

Religious confidence based on observing the Law presented a challenge that Paul continually confronted. He will return to this subject in both Romans 6 and 7.

Abraham and Faith

For Paul, right relationship with God has always been based on faith. It was an experience of grace for Abraham; it was also an experience of grace for Paul's readers. Indeed, because of a faith-response to God, Paul's readers, then and now, are truly the inheritors of the promises made to Abraham, for he is the father of all who have faith (4:16–25). Jews took pride in their physical descent from Abraham. But for Paul, it was spiritual descent that mattered. Relationships within the family of God are based on faith *only*. All those who have faith are Abraham's true descendants (4:16).

That unique relationship is discussed at length in 4:17–25. Abraham is seen here as a type—a forerunner or a foreshadowing—of the Christian believer. Abraham had faith in the One who could bring life out of death (the quickening of the dead). Specifically, Abraham took God at His word that he would be a father although he and Sarah had tried unsuccessfully for years to have a child and were now too old to have children. As far as the reproductive capacities of their aged bodies were concerned, they were "as good as dead" (verse 19, NIV). Yet Abraham believed God when he was told that he would be the father of many nations. He hoped against hope, beyond all the expectations that a reasonable human being might anticipate (4:18–19).

Children are sometimes disillusioned with well-meaning parents who constantly make great promises but are unable to carry through on those promises. But Abraham was confident that God was able to deliver what He had promised (4:21). He "did not waver in unbelief" (4:20, NASB). And because of that faith, he was declared righteous by God.

This is not limited to Abraham, though. He has simply foreshadowed the experience of Christians who also trust in the One who is able to bring life out of death. For Abraham, life out of death was the bringing forth of a child from bodies too old to bear children. For Christians, life out of death has taken on new meaning because of the Cross and Resurrection of Jesus. Here is the ultimate act of bringing life out of death. Faith for the Christian is centered not in a book, a creed, or a proposition of any kind. It is a response to the One who has demonstrated for all time that He can bring life out of death. He raised from the dead the crucified Lord.

Verse 25 contains two parallel statements: Jesus was delivered (put to death) for our offenses; He was raised for our justification. For Paul, these are inseparable aspects of one event. He wants us to see clearly that the death and resurrection of Jesus constitute one process whereby our sins are forgiven and we are made right with God.

From beginning to end, salvation becomes reality only through faith—the "meaning of salvation" Paul has illustrated by the great word pictures of Romans 3. And the "example of faith" he has described by recounting the experience of

Abraham in Romans 4. What we could not do for ourselves, God has provided in Jesus Christ: justification by faith.

Almighty God, You said in Your Word, "The just shall live by faith." Help me to walk in the faith You've given me. Amen.

He was delivered over to death for our sins and was raised to life for our justification.

—Romans 4:25 (NIV)

I sat in church on Easter, observing people greeting one another, the beauty of the lilies, and the sound of the trumpets beginning the first hymn. But something was holding me back from totally entering into joy. I knew the reason: I didn't do Lent very well.

This year, I wanted to be more in-the-moment responsive to Jesus and obedient to His nudges to do or not do at least one different thing every day. Like not voicing that negative thought. Or giving more grace to that annoying person. Or reading instead of watching that mind-numbing TV program. But some days I made that negative comment anyway, or lacked the grace I meant to extend, or just plain forgot about Lent. So I entered church on Easter, feeling guilty about my inconsistent responses.

As the service progressed—through the words of the songs, confessions, prayers, and sermon—I began to experience a humbling awareness that I'd come to Easter exactly the way I should come, with a fresh understanding of how I so easily mess up. And I was freshly thankful that the truth of the Easter message is not about anything I do or earn, but about the powerful promise of forgiveness and hope and eternal life.

—*Carol Kuykendall*

Notes

Notes

Notes

The Results of Salvation (I): Freedom in Christ

Merciful Father, there was a time when
I lived in sin without Your peace or joy.
Thank You for freeing me—to serve You! AMEN.

Marketers often use the concept of "felt need" to promote their products. In simple terms, in their marketing pitches, marketers present a problem, one that many people can relate to, and then declare that their product is the remedy to that problem. Then they tell or show the reader or viewer how much better they will feel or how much better things will be once they have used the product. It's a simple three-act play— problem, remedy, relief.

Although Paul certainly was not writing such a marketing pitch, it is interesting to note that he shares with modern writers that basic format as he writes the epistle to the Romans. As we have already seen, he has given in 1:18–3:19 a detailed picture of the plight or predicament of humankind as sinners. Then in 3:20–4:25 he has described the remedy: Jesus. The solution to the problem of the human race is found in the salvation that God offers through Jesus Christ for those who by faith will accept it. Now, in much of the remainder of the letter, you could say that Paul concentrates on the relief: the results of that salvation experience, both from a theological perspective (chapters 5–8) and in light of its ethical consequences (chapters 12–15).

Sometimes commercials seem to spend more time describing the problem than they do noting the results of the desired action. In contrast, Paul does just the opposite. He devotes more space in his letter to depicting the outcome—the relief—of salvation than he does in describing either the problem of sin or the provision of God. This should come as no surprise, however. After all, he is writing to the Roman Christians, a group of people who have experienced both the problem and the remedy—the solution. To be complete, this letter of self-introduction, in which the author presents an overview of the gospel he proclaims, would demand such descriptions. But the discussion that would benefit his readers most would be of that facet of salvation that would best relate to their present experience. Consequently, he devotes the largest part of his letter to this theme.

So extensive is his discussion, in fact, that we must devote two of our lessons to his theological discussion of the results of salvation. We'll call them The Results of Salvation I (lesson 4) and The Results of Salvation II (lesson 5). Both lessons will concentrate on Paul's concept of the freedom that the believer finds in Christ: freedom from alienation from God and freedom from sin in this lesson; and freedom from the Law and freedom in the Spirit in lesson 5.

Freedom from Alienation (5:1–11)

Reconciliation

In our study of Romans 3, we found that Paul used great word pictures to illustrate his understanding of salvation. Those pictures—justification, redemption, and expiation—don't always connote the same image for us as they did for Paul's first readers. At least they do not have the same impact.

Slave market analogies and images taken from a religious system based on animal sacrifice just don't speak to us today with the same force that they did in the first century. For this reason, talk of justification doesn't have much impact on us, for we don't feel that we need to be made right.

In this lesson, however, Paul introduces yet another word picture for what God has accomplished in Christ (5:1–11). But this time the term speaks dramatically to our modern times! In Christ, we have been "reconciled" to God (5:10).

This is an idea that we can easily identify with. At almost every relationship level, alienation is a stark reality of modern life. There is alienation between nations, between social classes, between geographical areas of one country, between generations, between races, between sexes, between adherents of different political beliefs, and, frequently, within families. All of us have known the feeling of being isolated, cut off from others. Social media, which was expected to bring people together, often only polarizes us further. And all of us have experienced hostility from some person or group.

To have our plight as sinners described in terms of separation or alienation from God, then, is an analogy that we can readily understand. To describe our need for God in terms of being reconciled to Him is to speak to a situation we can easily understand. When Paul says that God has reconciled us to Himself, he conjures up for us an image of God's bridging a gap, of His breaking down barriers, of His overcoming hostility.

Whenever Paul speaks of reconciliation (see also 2 Corinthians 5:18 and following, Ephesians 2:13 and following, and Colossians 1:20 and following), he always describes an action of God—an action that God performs. In other words, we cannot reconcile ourselves to God; just the opposite is true. God is ever the "Reconciler"; we are always the "reconciled." This certainly magnifies Paul's concept of grace. The saving action of God is initiated by Him, and it is offered freely by Him to those who can do nothing to help themselves. In Jesus Christ, He comes to mankind to reconcile people to Himself.

Although the term does not appear until verse 10, reconciliation seems to be the key concept of the first eleven verses of chapter 5. Peace with God (5:1) is the result of reconciliation, and atonement (5:11) is a synonym for it. Atonement, or "at-one-ment," refers to the quality of being at one with God—reconciled to Him.

The results of reconciliation (5:1–5)

The *therefore* of verse 1 ties this chapter with what has gone before. Someone has quipped that when we find a "therefore" in scripture, we ought to find out what it is there for. Here it introduces the logical consequences of what Paul has previously described: "for all have sinned and fall short of the glory of God" (3:23, ESV). Through sin, the human race is separated from God; in Christ, God has provided for our salvation, and that becomes reality for us, through faith. For everyone who accepts this salvation (Paul considers his Roman readers in that group), here are the results.

The first consequence of the salvation experience, whether it is described in terms of reconciliation, justification, redemption, or expiation, is peace with God (5:1). Although peace implies an absence of hostility, it signifies something more. Peace is that state of inner well-being that we enjoy through a proper relationship with God. Remember, the word *peace* is mentioned earlier in Paul's greeting to the Romans (1:7). There Paul intimated that true peace is enjoyed only by those who are recipients of God's grace.

A second consequence of the salvation experience is access to God (5:2). Ancient people did not feel that they had immediate access to their rulers. In the Old Testament story of Esther, the beautiful young queen came to the door of the king's chambers, but she was not given access until he pointed his scepter toward her (Esther 5:1–2). Access in this situation was limited, determined by whim. Access to God's grace, though, is unlimited for those whom He has reconciled. God is always available.

The third consequence of the salvation experience is hope (5:2–5). Hope is not just wishful thinking. Rather, it is a confidence or an assurance that is grounded in the reality of God's love. Specifically, the hope Paul mentions is that of sharing the glory of God, which humankind lost as a result of sin (3:23).

Paul then goes on to explain that this hope arises in hardship—it is produced as the result of a series of experiences that confront the Christian: Tribulation produces patience, which produces experience, which produces hope (5:3–4). While the exact word choice for *hardship* varies across our translations as "tribulations" (KJV, NASB), "sufferings" (ESV, NIV), and "hardship (distress, pressure, trouble)" (AMP), it produces endurance, patience, or perseverance, the ability to handle whatever difficulties may arise.

It is interesting that the biblical writers, echoing the teachings of Jesus (as in Matthew 5:11, for example), expected difficulties or suffering to be the lot of the Christian believer. This stands in stark contrast with the "gospel of success" that we hear so much about today. This is especially true when we are encouraging people to make generous tithing pledges or trying to pass the budgets of our churches. At such times we tend to promise that God will bless financially those who give to Him. Instead of financial gain, however, the New Testament seems to emphasize that the Christian will experience times of suffering and tribulation. But this is not a dismal, pessimistic view of life, for it is these experiences that build character, which in turn produces hope. Here the teaching of Paul is very similar to that of James (James 1:2) and Peter (1 Peter 1:6). Easy times are not the best soil for spiritual growth.

The reality of reconciliation (5:6–11)
These verses clearly demonstrate that reconciliation is entirely the work of God. While we were weak, without strength,

Christ died for us—the ungodly (5:6). When we could do nothing for ourselves, God acted. Even though we were estranged from Him, while we were sinners, says Paul, Christ died for us (5:8).

In the Gospels, Jesus is pictured as One who associated with sinners. In the Gospels, we saw Him socializing again and again with them and ministering to them. And in explaining this to His critics, Jesus used the analogy of a physician: "It is not the healthy who need a doctor, but the sick" (Mark 2:17, NIV).

Though virtual doctor visits are now relatively common for some conditions or ailments, physicians still do not generally practice medicine from a distance. They come into contact with those who need them. In vivid detail, the Gospel writers picture a Jesus who made it a point to reach people at their level of need, and He met them on their own ground.

Paul conveys some of this same idea here. Christ died for us while we were sinners. Christ did not suggest that we try to get better on our own before He would do something for us. After all, there was nothing we could do! Yet while we were weak, while we were still sinners, while we were enemies (5:10), He did something for us: He died on the Cross to reconcile us to Himself.

We learn, too, from our scripture lesson that reconciliation has future implications. Because we have been reconciled, we shall be saved from the wrath of God (5:9). Since His love and His wrath are two sides of the same coin, as we learned in lesson 2, we are free from His wrath because we have accepted His love.

Christic and Adam

Christ and Adam

But how can the action of one Man have such a wide-reaching effect? To answer this question, which Paul perhaps thought his readers might ponder, he turns to an analogy (5:12–21). Just as one man, Adam, had unleashed sin in the world through his disobedience in the Garden of Eden, Jesus Christ was able to reverse the effects of sin in the world "by becoming obedient to the point of death, even death on a cross" (Philippians 2:8, ESV).

Now this analogy in no way implied that these two were equal. Christ is superior to Adam. The consequence of Adam's action was death (5:12, 17); the result of Christ's act of reconciliation is life (5:17). Through his disobedience, Adam brought sin into the world. Yet, through Christ's obedience, grace came to the human race (5:15). Adam's sin provided the basis for condemnation. Christ's free gift, on the other hand, has brought righteousness—right standing for the human race before God (5:18). In a very real sense, Christ has reversed the sin of Adam and its consequences.

The disobedience of Adam was serious. Because of it, sin gained a foothold in the world. And, according to Paul's understanding, death became a reality because of sin. Much misunderstanding of Paul's thought over the centuries has been fostered by a poor translation of verse 12. When the original Greek language was translated into Latin in the late fourth century, the clause "for that all have sinned" was incorrectly rendered "in whom all have sinned." This mistranslation suggested to St. Augustine and others after him that all humankind participated in Adam's sin and that everyone will die as a result of Adam's failure. But this misrepresents Paul's position.

Interpreting verse 12 to mean that God punishes all of humankind by death because one man sinned suggests that God is unfair. And this is almost certainly not what Paul meant. Although he insists that Adam introduced both sin and death into the world, he states clearly that everyone dies because of his or her own sin, which is how most, if not all, of our English translations render it: "because all sinned." Each person repeats the sin of Adam in his or her own experience.

At the same time, Paul does not think that we are saved collectively. We are saved individually as we respond in faith to God's grace. The scope of salvation is universal in potential; Christ died for all humankind. Practically, though, it is limited to those who accept it. God does not coerce. He does not force salvation on anyone. But He freely gives it to every person who accepts it.

In the same way, Paul doesn't think that all of humankind participates in the consequences of Adam's sin *collectively*. Each person is held accountable for his or her own sin, and each person dies as a consequence of his or her own action. (See the similar teaching in James 1:13–15.)

Sin, for Paul, is not identical with transgression. Transgression is a conscious violation of the Law or of a commandment. Adam transgressed because he disobeyed a specific commandment of God. Generally, though, transgression is conceived of in relation to the Law. This means that the people between

Adam and Moses did not transgress, for there was no Law. But they did sin, and they died (5:13–14).

Now the whole process has been reversed by the "one Man" (verse 15, NASB), Jesus Christ. Through His obedience, He has brought grace, righteousness, and life into the world for those who believe (5:21).

For Paul there are two streams of humanity, each issuing from a different source. Every person is a member of one stream or the other. A person is either in Christ or in Adam. Those who belong to the stream of Adam are characterized by disobedience, sin, transgression, condemnation, and death. But some have changed streams by their faith in Jesus Christ, and these people are destined for eternal life.

Freedom from Sin (6:1–23)

The Analogy of Baptism

In 5:20 Paul suggests that the giving of the Law caused the offense against God to increase. Humankind had sinned apart from the Law, but after the Law was given, the plight of the human race was compounded. Not only are we guilty of sin apart from the Law, but we are also guilty of the sin of violating the Law. Paul's good news, though, is that where sin flourished, grace increased even more.

This understanding led Paul's opponents to a logical, but erroneous, conclusion about his teaching. If an increase of sin in the world causes a proportionately greater outpouring of grace, then we might conclude that it is our "Christian duty" to sin much so that grace might be multiplied! Paul addresses this errant thinking in chapter 6.

After posing the question as his imaginary opponent might state it (6:1), Paul responds with the strongest negative answer possible. "God forbid" (KJV) that one should consider sinning so that grace could function better. How could a Christian even think of sin as an option since he or she has died to it?

In the previous discussion of Adam and Christ, Paul indicated that Adam's sin resulted in death because that is the price that must be paid for sin. With confidence, though, he has also insisted that Christ's death has paid the ultimate penalty for sin. In fact, Christ's death paid the price for "the sins of the whole world" (1 John 2:2, ESV). We need only believe in Him and receive that gift of salvation (see John 1:12; Acts 16:31). In His death, sin itself was overcome and defeated "once for all" (Hebrews 7:27, ESV).

The defeat of sin becomes effective for us, though, only in our acceptance of the grace or free gift that has been offered to us. Grace is potentially available for all, but it becomes reality only for those who avail themselves of the opportunity.

In a similar way, for those who accept Christ's offer of salvation, the experience of His death to sin becomes effective. Through salvation, they participate in His death and its consequences. This experience is effectively demonstrated in baptism (6:1–14).

Christian baptism was a rite borrowed from John the Baptist. He in turn probably borrowed the practice from mainstream Judaism. The Jews used the rite as one of three requirements for a Gentile who was a proselyte, a convert, to their religion. In addition to circumcision and the offering of a sacrifice, the convert had to be baptized.

For the Jews, this act evidently symbolized more than one reality. First, it symbolized the death of an old way of life and the beginning of a new life. So totally different was the person who was baptized into Judaism that technically he could even marry his sister—as a new person he was no longer physically related to her! Although we don't know that this practice was ever actually carried out, the rabbis did insist that it was a possibility.

Second, baptism for the convert also symbolized identification with ancient Israel. When these people entered the promised land of Canaan after their wilderness wanderings, they had to cross the Jordan. According to Jewish belief, the people who crossed the Jordan at this time not only crossed it for themselves but also for all of their descendants. This meant that all Jews had effectively entered into the inheritance promised by God.

The ancestors of the proselytes had not crossed the Jordan in their behalf, however. Consequently, as they entered into Judaism, baptism was a way of identifying with the experience of ancient Israel. It was a symbolic crossing of the Jordan for them.

John the Baptist radically reinterpreted the practice, however. He insisted that everyone needed "to cross the Jordan" for himself or herself. It did not matter that the Jews had had ancestors who had been properly related to God. Everyone needed to relate to God individually. For John, this was a matter of faith, not family descent.

Paul found the symbolism of Jewish proselyte baptism as reinterpreted by John to be particularly appropriate for the Christian. In the baptismal waters the Christian also identified with a significant event of the past—not Israel's crossing of the Jordan but Jesus's death on the Cross (6:3). Just as Jesus died to sin, so do we as we profess our faith in Him and demonstrate that faith in baptism. Furthermore, as the Jewish proselyte felt himself to be a new person after baptism, so also Paul believes that the Christian undergoes the same kind of experience. Consequently, we have the reference to the death of "our old self" (6:6, NASB).

For Paul, baptism effectively symbolized this new beginning of the believer with Christ. It acts out the burial of the self that is alienated from God and dominated by sin. It demonstrates the newness of life that characterizes the one who has been reconciled to God (6:4). The Early Church baptized believers immediately after their profession of faith in Jesus. For them, baptism effectively marked the transition from the old life to the new.

We must remember at this point that Paul has not mentioned baptism simply so that he can set forth his understanding of the theological significance of the rite. He mentions it to support his argument that sin no longer dominates the believer. Rather, the believer's "death" to sin (6:11) is effectively demonstrated in baptism. For this reason, the true believer should not toy at all with the idea of sinning so that grace may abound (6:1).

It is important for us to understand, however, that Paul does not suggest that the believer will never again commit individual sinful acts. Rather, he insists that the believer is no longer dominated by sin (6:14).

The Analogy of Slavery

To clarify his point, Paul turns to a second analogy: slavery (6:15–23). He has already used this concept more than once to picture spiritual realities. By using the term *redemption* in 3:24, he suggested that a person who was enslaved to sin has been emancipated by the atoning death of Jesus. Yet earlier he had identified himself to his readers as a servant (slave) of Christ Jesus (1:1). For Paul, the act of faith on the part of the believer results in a paradox. The Christian is set free from slavery to sin, but in that act he or she becomes the slave of another—Jesus Christ. True freedom is found in being a servant to Christ.

Paul capitalizes upon this idea in these verses to buttress his assertion that a true believer in Christ is no longer under the dominion of sin. Such a person has changed masters. Jesus had used the same analogy, stressing that no man can serve two masters (Matthew 6:24), and Paul now makes a similar point. Enslavement to sin results in uncleanness, iniquity, and ultimately death. When a person changes masters, there is a resultant change in lifestyle. The consequences of enslavement to Christ are righteousness, holiness, and ultimately eternal life (6:19–22).

Uncleanness and iniquity belong to the old master. Any behavior characterized by these qualities cannot be entertained or tolerated (6:21) by the believer who has been redeemed through Christ's death on the Cross and set apart for service to the Lord.

In chapter 6 Paul has argued both that the Christian is effectively dead to sin and that the believer is a slave who has been purchased by a new Master. Now he concludes with a meaningful contrast that again points out the absurdity of the question he raised in 6:1, as he states emphatically, "For the wages of sin is death; but the gift of God is eternal life through Jesus Christ our Lord" (6:23, KJV).

The Christian should not consider, even for a moment, the possibility of sin as a lifestyle. Sin, after all, is like a careful employer who pays a guaranteed wage: death. Death is precisely what we bargain for when we make a deal with sin; it is the only salary or wage that sin can pay. Anyone who strikes such a bargain receives exactly what is deserved.

By contrast, however, Paul sees God not as the scrupulous employer that pays an employee only what has been earned but as the loving One who gives the gift of eternal life.

Here, then, is a consequence of salvation. We are transformed into people whose lives are completely under the control of Jesus Christ. This is not to say that our every action is acceptable and right in God's sight, but as redeemed children of God and as members of His fellowship, we are irrevocably committed to Him.

Dear God, thank You for this lesson. May it help me remember who I am in You. Day by day, moment by moment, remind me of the truths I've learned. AMEN.

Therefore, since we have been justified by faith, we have peace with God through our Lord Jesus Christ.

—Romans 5:1 (ESV)

The other morning at church, the pastor began a series of sermons on faith with the first definition that made sense to me after decades of atheism. "Now faith is being sure of what we hope for and certain of what we do not see" (Hebrews 11:1, NIV). Actually, the wording of the version he read was somewhat different from my husband's earlier edition of the NIV: "Now faith is confidence in what we hope for and assurance about what we do not see." Perhaps that's why the pastor understood this definition to be about *confidence* and *assurance*, whereas, for the struggler I once was, faith was synonymous with *hope*.

I had hoped throughout the decades of my atheism. And though by now I've believed in God longer than I hadn't, my faith is still more reliant on hope than certainty. Faith just doesn't come naturally for me. I have to reach for it daily, and the reaching is all about hope that what I've been taught, what I relearn daily, what Scripture routinely claims, is true: God loves us so much He sent His Son to save us from ourselves.

So it surprised me to come to a full turnaround in my understanding of the passage. I saw, with certitude, that my grasping hope wasn't faith exactly, though it has sufficed these many years. Rather, my faith came about through God's response to my hope—His willingness to be grasped and held and depended upon. I marveled at our invisible God's power to claim us for His own.

Thank You for Your love, Father, and the convincing authority of Your words.

—*Patty Kirk*

Notes

Notes

Notes

The Results of Salvation (II): Law and the Spirit

Dear Lord, thank You for Your Holy Spirit, who lives in me, and whose whole objective is to glorify You! AMEN.

We saw in our last lesson that God's provision for sinful people—salvation by grace through faith—results in freedom from alienation from God and freedom from the awesome power of death. But now in this lesson, Paul turns our attention to two additional aspects of Christian liberation. First, he discusses in chapter 7 the fact that as Christians, we are set free from the Law. And then to complete his discussion, in chapter 8 he concentrates on the context of Christian freedom: life in the Spirit.

Freedom from the Law (7:1–25)

For Paul as a person, the idea that salvation through Christ gave him freedom from the Law was most significant. The strict and pious Judaism in which he had been raised had a great reverence for the Law as God's special revelation for the Hebrew people. The Law dictated their daily lifestyle. It expressed both what they should and should not do. And it defined specific behavior that was acceptable to God and conducive to good relations with other people. For a Jew, then, the Law was of paramount importance, and right standing before God was determined by careful observance of the Law.

Before his conversion, Paul had taken great pride in the Law. In fact, he was so conscientious in following the rules laid down by the Jewish Law that he could say with all honesty that he was "blameless" (Philippians 3:6, ESV). So, for him to suggest that in Christ the Christian—even a Jewish Christian—was set free from the Law was a major truth even though it went against all of his earlier teaching.

The Analogy of Marriage

Back in chapter 6, Paul used the analogies of baptism and of slavery to illustrate the Christian's freedom from sin. Here he uses another word picture to describe freedom from the Law (7:1–6). Although his readers would include both Jews and Gentiles who have become Christians, he assumes that they are all familiar with the Law (7:1). Consequently, he takes his analogy from the Law to say something about the Law.

According to the legal code of the Old Testament, a woman was bound to her husband in marriage for as long as he lived. Now, it is true that divorce was possible for a man under the Law, but Paul is not discussing that issue here. Rather, his point is that death terminates the marriage relationship. After the death of a husband, the wife was free to marry again, and in forming a new marital relationship, she would in no way be guilty of any impropriety (7:3).

By way of comparison, then, Paul suggests that the Christian had formerly been "married" to the Law. But when the Christian "died to the Law," through the death of Jesus, then he or she was free to marry another—specifically, Christ (7:4).

At this point, though, Paul's analogy seems to break down. In his illustration, the first husband parallels the Law, the wife equals the Christian, and the new husband is Christ. But in reality it is not the Law that has died; it is the Christian who has died to it. Without getting bogged down in the analogy, though, we can appreciate Paul's main point: a death terminates one relationship and opens the way for another to be formed.

Paul then moves on to make the point that because of the death to the old way of life that the Christian has experienced in accepting Christ (see 6:1–4), the Christian is also dead to the Law. And a new relationship with Christ takes its place. This new "marriage" relationship is to bear "fruit for God"— be productive for God—in contrast with the "fruit that results in death" produced in the old relationship.

Now, when Paul uses the term "living in the flesh" (7:5, ESV), he is not simply referring to physical life, for he is writing to Christians who are no longer "living in the flesh" even though they continue to be physically alive. Rather, "flesh" should be seen here in contrast with "spirit," a concept that Paul will develop further in Romans 8.

Many people today tend to accept the Greek idea that a person is divided into two opposing parts—flesh and spirit—that are at war with each other. Paul, however, is thoroughly Jewish in his background and thought. He accepts the Hebrew concept of a human life as a totality. According to this understanding, we do not *have* a soul imprisoned in a body of flesh. We *are* a soul, a total personality—a whole person. The foundation for this truth is laid in the creation story: ". . . and man *became* a living soul" (Genesis 2:7, KJV; italics added for emphasis); "a living person" (NASB). The Amplified Version captures the essence of the way Paul saw the makeup of a person: ". . . became a living being [an individual complete in body and spirit]."

In other words, in creation we were not given a soul; we became a soul.

Although Paul frequently uses terms that we might think refer to only a part of human nature—flesh, body, spirit, mind, soul—he is usually referring to the total person from a particular perspective. For example, in this part of Romans, Paul generally uses the term "spirit" to refer not to a part of a person but to the *whole* person properly related to God. "Flesh," on the other hand, refers to a person separated from God. From this we see that a person apart from God lives "according to the flesh," but in Christ, a person lives "according to the spirit."

As we begin to catch what Paul is actually saying in verse 5, we see that he comes to a rather radical conclusion: the "old self" that was married to the Law and was stimulated by sinful passions produced "fruit" that resulted in death. This underscores the relationship between the Law and sin and death!

But the "new self" in union with Christ produces fruit for God: holy living—a life lived for Christ. Jesus used a horticultural metaphor of "trees" and "fruit" when He taught, "You will recognize them by their fruits" (Matthew 7:20, ESV). But Paul now uses the word *fruit* for another analogy and likens it to "offspring"—that which is produced in a marriage relationship.

In other words, he is saying that people are known by the "fruit" they bear—the results that come from their way of life.

As Christians who are experiencing new life in Christ, we are called to be productive in our lifestyle. We were not saved to sit and be entertained but to make a difference in our world. We praise, and rightly so, the legacies of people like Mother Teresa for her selfless work among the sick and dying; Bishop Desmond Tutu because he laid his life on the line in the cause of human justice; and former President Jimmy Carter, who put on work clothes and gave his time and sweat working with Habitat for Humanity to produce better housing in the impoverished areas of our cities.

We honor those who work on Jesus's behalf today to make a better life for people here at home and around the world, who work tirelessly behind the scenes in ways that are crucial but often escape our notice.

But these people should not be the exception. Every Christian is called to produce "fruit for God" in his or her particular spheres of influence. It may be serving in a food bank or soup kitchen, cooking or delivering food for Meals on Wheels, serving as a volunteer in a hospital or nursing home, or just listening to the hurts of a friend or neighbor who is struggling with an overwhelming problem.

It is in the giving of our help and talent and resources—of ourselves—that we produce "offspring"—"fruit" for God. And it is this very idea that Paul wants to get across to his readers in Rome and to us.

Paul includes one more illustration in verse 6. The Law, he says, from which we are now released, is what had held us captive. The same analogy of enslavement that he had used to picture the reality of sin in 6:15 and following he now employs to describe the Law. He is saying that Christian believers experience the freedom of the Spirit because they have been freed from the letter of the Law. You will notice that we capitalized "Spirit" in that last sentence. Paul can use a word in more than one way. As we saw earlier, when he uses "spirit" to refer to a human being, he is describing a total person properly related to God. But, of course, he also uses that word to refer to the Spirit of God. Capitalizing the first letter of a word to indicate that it refers to deity is a fairly modern technique that is not found in the Greek texts of Paul's letters. So, in capitalizing the word *Spirit* here, we are, in a way, *interpreting* Paul's use of the word.

Paul will explain this concept of life in the Spirit more fully in Romans 8. And this sixth verse is a good introduction to that chapter. But before Paul can move on to his main point, he feels compelled to pause here and talk about the relationship between sin and the Law. If we were writing this in our style today, we would probably put parentheses around verses 7–25 because they seem to be a digression. This digression, though, is unavoidable. Paul has drawn a vivid parallel between sin and the Law in verses 1–6. Now he needs to explain more fully just what he means.

The Law and Sin
As we read this parenthetical paragraph, we have to ask ourselves, "Does Paul imply that the Law and sin are to be treated as equal?" By no means! Again Paul uses the strongest

possible negative answer to refute such an idea, "Is the law sin? *God forbid*" (7:7, KJV; italics added for emphasis). Even though he will not deny that there is a relationship between the two, he never suggests that the Law, God's special revelation to Israel—His chosen people—is anything but "holy, and just, and good" (7:12, KJV).

In describing the relationship between the Law and sin, Paul makes a grammatical shift in this part of our scripture lesson to the use of the first-person pronoun *I*. Bible students and teachers through the centuries have debated the meaning of this. Several questions emerge as we reflect on these verses. Is Paul describing his own experience? Is he speaking for the Jews as a race? Or is he perhaps saying that this is a universal experience? If his comments are autobiographical, is Paul talking about his present or his pre-conversion experience?

The difficulty with all of this is that it is further complicated by Paul's shift in his verb tenses beginning with verse 14. In verses 7–13 he uses the past tense. Then in verses 14–25 he shifts to the present tense. With this in mind, we then must ask, Do the former verses reflect his earlier experience, while the latter verses speak to his present dilemma?

Without getting bogged down in a detailed analysis of all the possibilities, let's take a look at what Paul has done here. First, the shift to the pronoun *I* is significant, though it might not mean that Paul is simply giving *his* experience alone. Rather, he is speaking for *every person* (himself included), for, especially in verses 7–13, he is describing the process involved in Adam's sin when he ate the forbidden fruit in the Garden of Eden. The Genesis story tells us that Adam was free from sin.

Then one day God laid down a law: "You are free to eat from any tree in the garden; but you must not eat from the tree of the knowledge of good and evil. . ." (Genesis 2:16–17, NIV). Then the serpent entered the scene, and the "thou shalt not" (KJV) became a temptation. Here we see one of the subtleties of human nature at work: When something is forbidden, it becomes strangely desirable. We've all experienced it.

For example, when you walk into a freshly painted room, you're probably not particularly tempted to touch the walls until you see the sign that reads Wet Paint. Do Not Touch. In reality, what is intended to warn us against bumping into the freshly painted wall and ruining our clothes actually provokes the desire to touch the wall!

Similarly, Paul indicates that he never thought about coveting as such until he heard the commandment, "You shall not covet" (7:7, NIV). It was then that sin, taking advantage of the commandment, deceived and defeated him. In other words, the Law provided sin the opportunity to work—it served as a catalyst for evil.

From all of this, however, we see that even though the Law came as a revelation from God, it is partial and incomplete; the final, perfect, and complete revelation of God has come in Jesus Christ. By faith in Him we receive the salvation that sets us free not only from the ineffectiveness of the Law but also from the power of sin that uses the Law to achieve its own purposes.

As we continue to reflect on what Paul is doing or not doing in these particular scripture verses, let's focus our attention on two additional points.

First, it's unlikely that Paul is giving an autobiographical account here of the feelings and frustrations he felt while he was under the Law—before his conversion. We have already noted and commented on his claim in Philippians 3:6 that he was blameless under the Law. That certainly doesn't seem to imply a feeling of hesitancy, uncertainty, or frustration, as is expressed in these verses (7:7–25). Instead, these give us an idea from a post-conversion perspective of what life apart from Christ is really like.

Second, though there may be differences of opinion on this point, it is also unlikely that Paul is describing the frustration of his *present* Christian experience. This would seem to contradict what Paul has already said in Romans 6 about being dead to sin. It also seems to contradict what he says later in Romans 8 about the victory the Christian experiences in the Spirit.

It seems that when we consider what has gone before and what follows, Paul is writing from the perspective of a Christian, and he is describing the experience of every person apart from Christ—one who is not converted. At the same time, it is also the experience of the Christian who attempts to live in his or her own strength and not "in the Spirit." For anyone who has tried "to go it alone," so to speak, Paul's words strike a responsive chord.

In the remainder of this parenthetical portion, we have a vivid description of ineffective intentions (7:14–25). Paul's word pictures portray the frustrations of a person who knows the right thing to do but invariably ends up doing just the opposite. Here, too, some view this as Paul's confession of his own struggle as a Christian. But, again, in view of what Paul writes in Romans 8 about the power of the Spirit in the life of the Christian, this interpretation is not consistent. It seems possible that the non-Christian could experience this conflict of knowing the good but choosing the evil, of intending one thing but doing the other.

For example, the pagan Roman and Greek poets obviously were familiar with this struggle between good and evil. In *Metamorphoses* Ovid wrote, "I see the right way and approve it, but follow the wrong." It is quite likely that Paul was intimately familiar with these very words, as Ovid preceded him by just a few years, and Tarsus, where he grew up, was one of the intellectual centers of the Greek and Roman world.

Earlier in his epistle to the Romans, Paul discussed God making Himself known to humankind in creation (1:19–20) and in conscience (2:14–15). And now he has just commented on the relationship between the Law and sin. Consequently, from all of this we can see that the struggle described in this part of our lesson refers to the experience of any person who has not accepted Jesus Christ as the Savior and Lord of life.

Throughout Romans 7 sin seems to be described as a person or spirit (see verses 8–9, 11, 13, 17, 20). And Paul certainly takes it seriously as a powerful force that overwhelms and enslaves a person. But he shouldn't be misunderstood here. The power of sin becomes effective when a person gives it a foothold in his or her own life. This simply means that a person dominated by sin is not an innocent victim. It is the person, not sin as some outside force, that is held accountable for his or her actions. Verses 17 and 20 could be taken at face value to mean that sin, not the individual person, is responsible for the evil in one's life. But Paul's earlier discussion of the sinfulness of humankind (1:18–3:20) indicates that the real responsibility lies within each person. And to properly understand these verses in chapter 7, we must interpret them within the context of everything that Paul writes. The lesson for us comes through clearly: sin is no scapegoat that can be blamed for our problems and our waywardness. Rejection of Christ and living a sinful life is a definite choice made by a person.

The climax of this long parenthetical statement (7:7–25) comes with the anguished cry of despair, "O wretched man that I am! who shall deliver me from the body of this death?" and the glimmer of hope, "I thank God through Jesus Christ our Lord" (7:24, 25, KJV). And that sets the stage for the long discussion of the triumph of the Spirit in Romans 8. Apart from Christ, there is no hope. The frustrations of knowing what is right but choosing what is wrong can be resolved only in Christ. From Paul's perspective, God's revelation of Himself in creation, in conscience, and even in the Law is inadequate and incomplete. These cannot deliver the "wretched man" from the dilemma of sin and the consequence of death (7:24). Our deliverance from the bondage of sin to a life of wholeness and victory can be found only in Jesus Christ.

Life in the Spirit (8:1–39)

Starting with Romans 5, Paul has discussed in detail the consequences of justification by faith—being made right with God. He has stated most of these consequences in terms of what the

Christian has been saved *from*—alienation, sin, and the Law. He now turns to a more positive perspective—not what we are saved from but what we are saved *for*: life in the Spirit.

In this eighth chapter we have Paul's most detailed discussion of the Spirit in the New Testament. It is interesting to note that in the first seven chapters of Romans, Paul used the word *spirit* only five times. And in the last eight chapters, 9 through 16, the word is used only eight times. But in chapter 8 Paul uses *spirit* twenty-one times. There was a purpose in Paul's use of language here that is very significant.

The Basis for Life in the Spirit—God's Saving Act

In the preceding part of our lesson (7:7–25), Paul vividly described part of the struggle experienced in a person's life apart from Christ. Here he examines the nature of a person's life *in* Christ. He opens by saying that for those who belong to Jesus Christ, "There is therefore now no condemnation" (8:1, ESV). This is the great Good News of the gospel! The word *now* moves us from BC to AD; it refers to the time *after* the triumph of Christ, which He experienced in His death and resurrection. Again, choosing a term from the legal system, Paul insists that "condemnation," which included the idea of punishment that followed sentencing in court, has been done away with. The Law had not been able to achieve this removal of condemnation. But in Jesus Christ, "God has done what the law, weakened by the flesh, could not do (8:3, ESV).

One of Paul's favorite phrases is used here in verse 1, "in Christ." This phrase is used to describe the relationship of the Christian believer with Christ, and it is used repeatedly in all of Paul's writings. But Paul also expresses this idea in another way when he speaks of Christ being *in us* (see 8:10, for example). "In Christ" and "Christ within" are not attempts to define a spatial relationship but a spiritual one. They are both descriptive of one experience.

Paul can also talk about the believer being in the Spirit (8:9) and the Spirit being in the believer. Not only is Paul using these two phrases to describe the same relationship, but he is also using them to describe the same experience as that which he calls "in Christ." "In Christ" and "in the Spirit" are the same for Paul, because for him "the Lord is the Spirit" (2 Corinthians 3:17, NASB).

When we understand Paul's identification of Christ and Spirit, we are better able to catch the meaning of verse 2: the Law (which should be interpreted as "principle" as we saw in 7:21) of the Spirit *is* the Law of life in Christ Jesus; it is this principle that has set us free from the law of sin and death.

This freedom was not possible under the Law; it became reality in God's action in Jesus Christ, who was sent "in the likeness of sinful flesh" (8:3, NIV). This last phrase was probably used to emphasize the sinlessness of Jesus. The word *flesh*, as we have seen, when used by Paul means life alienated from God by sin. Though Christ became a human being, He did not become sinful, nor was He alienated from God. Consequently, in describing the human Jesus, Paul uses the word *likeness* so that no one will misunderstand the sinlessness of Jesus.

Verse 3 uses a phrase often translated as "a sin offering" (NIV) or "as an offering for sin" (NASB). With those words, Paul says in this verse that God sent His own Son as a sinless human being to be a sin offering that settled the problem of sin once and for all. For people who are in Christ Jesus, there is no condemnation (8:1), but because of Christ Jesus sin is condemned!

What Christ accomplished was righteousness. This is the right standing before God that the Law demanded but was powerless to achieve (8:4).

Life in the Spirit and Life in the Flesh

Twice in the first four verses of chapter 8 Paul mentioned those who walk in the flesh and those who walk in the Spirit (8:1, 4). Now he makes an explicit comparison of the two (8:5–11).

Those who are "governed by the flesh" (verse 6, NIV) are those who are in hostile opposition to God (8:7). Their lives are "carnally minded" (KJV), focused on those desires and aspirations that are opposed to God (8:5), and their end is death (8:6).

On the other hand, people who live according to the Spirit are those who are right with God; their lives are focused on Him (8:5). The result of this lifestyle is life (as opposed to death) and peace (8:6). In fact, Paul explicitly states that the Spirit of the One who raised Jesus from the dead will also "give life to" (NIV) or "quicken" (KJV) everyone who lives according to the Spirit (8:11).

Who are these whose lives are dominated by the Spirit? They are all Christians, including Paul's readers (8:9), because the Spirit of God dwells within them. In fact, Paul insists that we cannot belong to Christ without having the Spirit of God dwelling in us.

You will notice in these verses that Paul uses different designations or titles when referring to the Holy Spirit: "Spirit of God," "Spirit of Christ" (8:9), and "his Spirit who dwells in you" (8:11, ESV). This emphasizes an important truth: when we speak of the Trinity, we should not think of God as three *separate* persons, one of whom can be accepted without receiving the other two. A believer cannot accept Christ, for example, without at the same time accepting the Father and the Spirit. The three are one. God cannot be received in installments. For Paul, anyone who does not have the Spirit does not belong to Christ in any way (8:9).

The Spirit and Sonship

One of the most beautiful pictures of God in Scripture is that of the loving Father. Paul uses that image here as he describes the relationship of the Christian with God (8:12–17). Just as the father in Jesus's parable of the prodigal son (Luke 15:11–32) refused to accept his returning son as a servant because he wanted him as a son, so God does not accept us as slaves but as children (8:15).

All analogies break down at some point, and we should not expect Paul to be rigidly consistent in his use of them. He was glad to identify himself earlier as a servant—slave—of Christ in Romans 1:1, but there he was referring to his total commitment to the Lord. Now, in these verses, he uses the slave analogy again, but from a different perspective. Here he is contrasting the roles of servant and son in a household, and his point is that God accepts believers as part of the family. What an awesome thought—we are members of God's family!

Specifically, Paul uses the analogy of adoption (8:15) to describe this relationship because he has just been talking about Jesus as God's own Son (8:3). We Christians are also God's children, but we are so by adoption. Adoption does not imply a second-class status in the family. Rather, it involves the deliberate choice of a child to bear the family name and to be heir to the family inheritance.

Evidence of this relationship with God comes from two sources. One is our own perception of God as "Abba" (8:15). This word is the Aramaic term of affection used to refer to one's father. In English its equivalent is something like "Daddy." It was this same word that Jesus used in His prayer life to address God. Now, because we are "in Christ," we can relate to God in the same intimate way. And because we can relate to God in this way, we are assured that we have indeed been adopted as His children.

The other proof or evidence of our special relationship with God comes from the testimony of the Holy Spirit within us (8:16). And since we are His children, we are His heirs, or more specifically, ". . . joint-heirs with Christ . . . that we may also be glorified together" (8:17, KJV). That is an electrifying promise, but it brings with it a reminder of suffering. Paul is saying that Jesus received glory through—in relation to—His suffering. If we then are joint heirs with Him, suffering of one kind or another will also be our lot and our path to glory. In a world where people are living "according to the flesh"—in opposition to God—hard times and suffering can be expected by everyone who lives "according to the Spirit."

Suffering and Hope

Paul moves on now to assure his first-century readers and us that, even though we may experience various forms of physical and mental suffering because of our faith, none of this is "worthy to be compared with the glory that is to be revealed to us" (8:18, NASB). The word *glory* used here takes us back to Paul's earlier discussion of sin, "All have sinned, and come short of the glory of God" (3:23, KJV). It was sin that robbed us of God's glory, but now because of the presence of the indwelling Holy Spirit, that glory is our hope!

Paul introduces a further thought in this part of our scripture lesson (8:19–21). Not only are we, as members of God's family, looking toward and hoping for God's glory, but it is also the hope of all of creation.

As he writes, Paul likely has in mind the creation story where the earth itself was cursed because of Adam's sin and the "fall" of all mankind (Genesis 3:17). The idea here is that even as the entrance of sin into the human race had a devastating effect on the world of nature, so the ultimate redemption of mankind through the completed work of Christ will then restore God's glory throughout the universe.

To increase the intensity of color in the picture Paul is drawing here, he then uses the metaphor of a woman in labor who groans for relief from the pain of childbirth (8:22) and likens it to the intensity of creation's longing to be free of the curse and restored to its original glory.

To understand what Paul wants us to get here is the recognition of the scriptural tension between the "now" and the "not yet." Salvation for Paul is a dynamic process. It began at some point in the past when the believer accepted God's grace. It is going on now and is yet to be completed at the end of time as we know and understand it. It is this process, for example, that explains the seeming change in Paul's thought from verse 15 to verse 23. In the earlier verse, he talked about adoption as something that *had taken place*. Now he speaks of it in terms of future hope. Every analogy for salvation is subject to the same "now, but not yet" tension. Adoption, which is the equivalent of redemption (8:23), has begun in the past, is in the process of going on now, and will be fully realized in the future.

To illustrate the same idea, Paul also uses an agricultural picture. The salvation we have experienced in Christ is the "firstfruits of the Spirit" (8:23, NIV). "Firstfruits" were literally what the name implied: the first fruits of the harvest. In ancient Israel the first portion of anything made or grown was offered to God in thanksgiving and as a sample or a foretaste of what was to come. What we have experienced in the Spirit is genuine, but it is only a foretaste of what is to come.

That is our hope, and "through perseverance we wait eagerly for it" (8:25, NASB). Our hope is anchored in a God who will carry out His final plan of salvation for us and His created order.

The Spirit and Intercession

Paul mentions three "groanings" in chapter 8. Creation groans (8:22), we groan (8:23), and the Spirit groans (8:26). The first two groan for deliverance, but the Spirit groans in intercession for us. There are times when we simply don't know *how* to pray about a particular matter or issue. In times like this, when we are most uncertain, we can rely on the Spirit to intercede for us in a way that is consistent with His will (8:27). Paul assures us here that the Spirit of God within us appeals to God outside us in our behalf. What more could anyone ask for?

The Assurance of God's Love

Perhaps the best-known verse in all of Romans is 8:28, but it is often misunderstood. When we look at the events in our lives, in the lives of others, and in the world, it is difficult to accept the idea that everything that happens to us is God's will, even though there are those who interpret this verse that way.

Most translators today agree that the familiar word order of the King James translation of this verse should be rearranged, and this rearrangement appears in later translations. The first words in the Greek text, the position of emphasis, are the ones translated "for those who love God." Then, too, the subject of the sentence should be changed. Rather than stating the idea that all things work together for good—that is, all things just happen to work out for the best—the meaning should be expressed as it is in the New International Version: "in all things *God* works for the good of those who love him" (italics added for emphasis). This translation suggests that whatever may occur, God determines the ultimate outcome of the event. But even more than that, God determines the outcome for the good of those who love Him.

When we are confronted with tragic experiences, it is difficult to see how anything good can come from them. We can't possibly see how God could be working in those situations. But hindsight is twenty-twenty. It is only later that we can look back and affirm that indeed God was at work and that He did bring something good out of those experiences—though it was hard to see at the time.

That is Paul's message of assurance in this part of our lesson. Whatever tragic or painful events that may come our way in life, God is not frustrated and His purposes are not thwarted. He is active at such times and will cause good to happen for those who love Him, for those "who have been called according to his purpose" (verse 28, NIV). For the Christian, everything *does* work out for good.

Paul's last phrase in verse 28 introduces a long series of terms that describe God's actions toward the believer (8:29–30). Probably the most difficult to understand are "foreknow" and "predestinate." The freedom of the human will that Paul discusses at length in the next major section of Romans (chapters 9–11), and which we will study in our next lesson, should not be forgotten as we interpret these particular verses.

When Paul writes, "For those God foreknew he also predestined to be conformed to the image of his Son" (8:29, NIV), he is referring to those who have already responded positively to God. It is not that God predetermined who would accept Him. Rather, He knew beforehand and predetermined that those who did choose to accept Him would "be conformed to the image of his Son."

The remainder of Romans 8 stresses in poetic beauty the dynamic power of the love of God. Verse 31 is an apt summary of Paul's thought: "If God is for us, who can be against us?" (ESV). He then goes on to say that no matter what hardships and obstacles threaten to overwhelm us, "we

overwhelmingly conquer through Him who loved us"
(8:37, NASB). And, finally, absolutely nothing can "separate
us from the love of God that is in Christ Jesus our Lord"
(8:39, NIV).

For the Christians in Rome, this majestic summary of
Paul's understanding of what it means to be "in Christ" must
have given them the courage to handle the brutality that was
unleashed on them by the emperor and his henchmen. For us,
our commitment to Christ may not bring on attacks of physical violence and threat of death, although there are places in
the world where it is dangerous to be a Christian. Instead, our
opposition may be social or psychological or it may operate
behind a "religious" front. But from wherever it comes and
whatever shape it takes, we know that *if God be for us, who
can be against us? . . . We are more than conquerors through
Him that loved us. . . . Nothing can separate us from the love of
God, which is in Christ Jesus our Lord.*

---

*Abba Father, I rejoice in Your magnificent power and love.
You not only dwell in me in the person of the Holy Spirit,
but You also allow me to dwell in Christ. Help me live a life
that reflects my dwelling place. AMEN.*

For I do not do the good I want to do . . . .

—Romans 7:19 (NIV)

I walked into the living room to find Kemo, our seven-year-old golden retriever, comfortably stretched out on the white love seat. "Kemo, what do you think you are doing?" I asked in amazement. Not because he was on the love seat (this wasn't the first time) but because instead of jumping down at being discovered, he wagged his tail as if he was proud of himself.

I know this sounds weird—unless you are a dog person—but part of me wanted to laugh because I sometimes identify with him. The look on Kemo's face said, "I'm doing something I know you don't like, but I know you love me enough to forgive me."

I do that, too, especially with my husband. I show up late somewhere or continue looking at my laptop when he's talking to me or get annoyed with his slower walking pace. These are all things

I know I shouldn't do, but I trust that my husband, Lynn, loves me enough to forgive me again and again and again.

Lord, thank You for this reminder about taking someone's love and forgiveness for granted, including Yours.

—*Carol Kuykendall*

Notes

Notes

Notes

Israel and Christ: The Problem of the Rejection of the Jews

Loving Father, open my mind and heart to receive Your Word. AMEN.

The history of the church is filled with stories of Christians who have grieved because members of their families failed to accept God's offer of salvation. Perhaps the most notable example is Paul. His "family" was the Jewish people, and after his own conversion, he agonized over their failure to accept Christ as their Savior. Paul was proud of his Hebrew heritage and he was concerned that so few of his fellow Jews—"my kinsmen according to the flesh" (Romans 9:3, ESV)—had become Christians (9:1–5).

As a matter of fact, all of the first Christians had been Jews. The events and discussions in the first seven chapters of Acts deal with Christian Judaism; in those early days of the Jerusalem church, everyone who was a Christian was Jewish. But in the aftermath of the martyrdom of Stephen, Christianity broke through the barriers of race, religion, and nationalism to welcome Gentiles into its midst.

Now, a little more than twenty years after the Resurrection of Jesus, as Paul is writing this letter to the Romans, Gentiles outnumber Jews within the church. Paul's concern is not merely personal but also theological. Why have the people best prepared for the coming of the Messiah been so unwilling to accept Him? Why have the chosen people of God rejected the Son of God? Is God's will thwarted by their rejection? Or, more pointedly, does their rejection in some way suggest a failure on the part of God?

Paul discusses this issue in our lesson now as we look at the next three chapters of Romans (9–11). At first glance, we might feel that this section interrupts Paul's thought. We could easily jump from the end of chapter 8 to the beginning of chapter 12 without sensing that anything is missing. But what Paul says here does relate to his overall message; it is a variation of the theme of justification by faith—being righteous before God—and for this reason, it is important that we understand what Paul is saying.

Paul begins by stating his anguish at the rejection of Jesus by the Jews (9:1–3). He sets out immediately in these verses to assure his Jewish readers that even though he is busily involved with preaching and teaching the Good News of the gospel to Gentiles, he is not indifferent to the need of his fellow Jews—his "kinsmen"—to hear the truth. Many Christians throughout the centuries have agonized over unbelievers, but very few have equaled Paul's intense feeling. So great is his love and his desire for their salvation that he would willingly be "cursed" (NIV)—cut off from Christ—if it would mean *their* acceptance of Him (9:3). The intensity of Paul's love and concern for people who did not know Christ as their Savior is a colorful model for us today.

Then, in an expression of amazement at their unbelief, Paul lists the privileges that the Jews have enjoyed throughout their long history (9:3–5). Earlier in the letter (3:1–2) Paul, in response to the question, "What advantage, then, is there in being a Jew . . . ?" said, "Much in every way!" (3:1–2, NIV), and then he specifically mentioned that they had received the oracles of God. But here now he lists one privilege after another. They not only had the Law, but they were also God's chosen people. God had been active in their history and in their worship. How could they, who had had such a rich relationship with God, fail to respond to Him now?

The Sovereignty of God (9:6–29)

At the beginning of his discussion Paul rejects the idea that the failure of the Jews to receive Christ as the Messiah indicates some failure in the promise of God (9:6). Key to his thought here is the recognition of God's sovereignty— His absolute authority—as demonstrated in His election of Israel.

Election and Israel
Paul now points out that in the history of God's relationship with people, a selective process has always been at work (9:6–13). God's promise to Abraham and to his heirs, for example, was not merely to those physically descended from the patriarch. After all, Ishmael and his descendants were also sons of Abraham, but they were not "the children of the promise" (9:8, ESV), the ones through whom God worked to

achieve His purpose in the world. Rather, God's plans were at work through Abraham's son Isaac and his descendants (9:7).

But even in this line, the process of election continued to be exercised. Before the twins Jacob and Esau were born to Isaac and Rebecca, it was clear that God chose to work through Jacob (9:10–13). This selection was not based on the works or achievements of one over the other; the election was made before they were born (9:11).

And to emphasize the point, Paul quotes from Malachi: "Jacob I loved, but Esau I hated" (9:13, NIV). We need to understand that what is really implied here is that God preferred Jacob over Esau. The Hebrew words for *love* and *hate* do not convey the same meaning we usually give them, and the Amplified Bible rendering of Malachi 1:2–3 communicates this meaning: "Yet I loved Jacob (Israel); but [in comparison with My love for Jacob] I have hated Esau (Edom)."

In choosing Jacob to be the channel through which God would act to save humankind, He was exercising His intention to follow a plan best suited to the overall good of people. As Paul's Jewish readers would well understand, such decisions are not determined by the desires or actions of people but by God's eternal purposes.

Perhaps the best explanation for this idea is found in verse 6: "For not all who are descended from Israel belong to Israel" (ESV). Here Paul uses one word with two very different meanings just as he did with the term "Law" in chapter 7. The first "Israel" refers to the true people of God. The second refers to the patriarch himself. Not everyone, then, who is descended from Israel (Jacob) genetically is a part of the people of God. Instead, those who constitute the true Israel have been chosen by God. Here Paul is reacting to the assumption of the Jews that merely because they are descendants of Abraham they cannot be rejected by God. Although he does not mention the idea of faith at this point, we can infer from what Paul has said earlier that the ones whom God chooses are those who respond to Him in faith. This idea of God's sovereign choice will be balanced in the next chapter (11) by a discussion of the freedom of humankind.

In a practical sense, we learn from Paul's statement in these verses that God chooses or selects us because of our faith in Jesus Christ. It isn't our denominational heritage or our outward response to certain external rules or codes of behavior that qualifies us to be chosen as children of God—it is our faith and obedience to Him.

The Example of Pharaoh

We should remember from our earlier study that "just" and "righteous" are two ways of translating the same Greek word. Here then, in verse 14, the term "unrighteousness" (KJV) is better understood in our culture as "injustice," some form of which we see used in most modern translations. And this is the charge that could be levied against God if His choice has been arbitrary. That this is *not* the case is indicated by Paul's most emphatic negative: "God forbid!" (KJV).

At first glance, though, the next few verses (9:15–18) cite selections and examples from the Old Testament that seem to indicate something arbitrary, and therefore unjust, about God's elections—the choices He makes. There are several factors that we must keep in mind if we are to understand Paul at this point.

First, if God's election (choice) of one person over another or one race of people over another race of people is an indication that He is fickle, capricious, or unfair in the use of His sovereign power, the picture of God that emerges is contradictory to the portrayal that Paul developed in the previous chapters of Romans. God is seen here as the One who loves people and provides a means of salvation for them when they do not deserve it and when they are unable to do anything for themselves. Furthermore, the great emphasis on faith that has been found throughout the book of Romans indicates that God as sovereign does not coerce any person.

In other words, even though God of His own accord has come to us, we are not forced into relationship with Him. Rather, relationship becomes real only as we accept God's gracious gift. Now, from all this we can conclude either that Paul is inconsistent in his view of God *or* that Paul's meaning can only be understood by interpreting these difficult verses in light of the clear teaching of the whole book.

Second, the quotation from Exodus 33:19, "I will have mercy on whom I have mercy, and I will have compassion on whom I have compassion" (9:15, ESV), is originally set in the context of deliverance. God is no capricious tyrant who moves people about like pawns on a chessboard. Rather, the words dramatically demonstrate that He is "compassionate and merciful, slow to anger, and abounding in faithfulness and truth" (Exodus 34:6, NASB). Contrary to what the world at that time might have expected, God chose to bless an insignificant, unattractive, less-than-promising, undeserving band of slaves. He called them to be His people. The world would call this action ridiculous, but God's ways are not the world's. The words quoted by Paul do not point to an unjust despot but to One who rules with justice *and* love and mercy.

Third, the example of Pharaoh does not necessarily suggest a harsh determinism on the part of God in which He dictates who will and who will not follow Him. Instead, Paul seems to be stressing the power of God to determine the ultimate outcome of events. Pharaoh may have intended evil for the Israelites, but God found in the stubborn arrogance of this ruler an opportunity to demonstrate His power and to cause His name to "be declared throughout all of the earth" (9:17, KJV). Instead of defeating God's purpose, Pharaoh was used to accomplish it!

How similar this incident is to another Old Testament story set in Egypt. Joseph, you will remember, was sold into slavery by his jealous brothers, but God found in this vicious act a way to eventually save the Hebrew race and others from starvation (see Genesis 50:20).

One of the most problematic phrases in this part of our scripture lesson is in the concluding statement in verse 18. After Paul repeats the idea that God has mercy on whom He wills, he adds, "He hardens [the heart of] whom He wills" (AMP). This last word is certainly reminiscent of the story in Exodus about Pharaoh, for there it is frequently used to describe this Egyptian's response to God. Several times the Old Testament records that Pharaoh hardened his heart (Exodus 8:15, 32; 9:34), but in many other instances, it says that God hardened Pharaoh's heart (for example, Exodus 4:21; 7:3, 13). Evidently, both expressions refer to the same kind of experience. Who, then, is responsible for the hardening, God or Pharaoh?

Paul would probably say both. In the Exodus passages the hardening of Pharaoh's heart was a *response* to a demonstration of God's power. God was therefore ultimately responsible, for He had caused a situation in which Pharaoh had to react—either positively toward God (which could be called a "melting of his heart") or negatively against God. But Pharaoh was not without choice in the matter. Although God confronted him, forcing a decision from him, it was Pharaoh who decided for or against God. God in His sovereignty confronts us in such a way that we must decide either for or against Him. But in His sovereignty, God does not decide what the decision will be.

The Potter and the Pot

We may not wish to be confronted with a decision for or against God, but we do not have the right or the ability to decide not to choose, for we are created as individuals who must make choices. At this point, Paul uses another analogy—that of God as a potter and a human being as a pot. The pot cannot question the potter about why it is made the way that it is. "Shall what is formed say to the one who formed it, 'Why did you make me like this?'" (9:20, NIV). Of course, this analogy like all analogies is not completely satisfactory, for a person is not like an inanimate object. But it is sufficient for Paul to make his point.

There seems to be a slight shift in the analogy beginning with verse 22. When Paul begins to talk about vessels of wrath and vessels of mercy, he changes the image from what it was in verses 19–21. In the previous verses he talks of a potter and pot to describe the absolute right of God to make us creatures of choice. But then after verse 22 Paul seems to use pots (vessels) to picture human beings who have made that choice. The New International Version captures this sense with its wording: "the objects of his wrath." God puts up with the "vessels of wrath"—those who are disobedient to Him—for the sake of others who will respond positively in faith (9:22–23).

The point, of course, is that the Jews are the "vessels of wrath" or "objects of his wrath" whom God is putting up with for the sake of the Gentiles. Paul's ministry has verified this idea for him. As we were told in Acts, when Paul first went to a new city, he looked up the Jews in order to preach the gospel to them. But after they rejected him, he then turned to the Gentiles. The disobedience of the Jews had opened up possibilities for the winning of the Gentiles.

The selection of passages quoted in verses 25–29 (Hosea 2:23; 1:10; and Isaiah 10:22; 1:9) support Paul's conclusion: God in His sovereignty is free to choose a new people. His original choice of Israel did not guarantee that every Israelite would be saved. Only the *faithful* remnant would see salvation (9:27). And Gentiles who had not been called His people would be called "children of the living God" (9:26, KJV). God is not defeated by Israel's rejection!

The Freedom of the Will (9:30–10:21)

The Stone of Stumbling

With this last paragraph (9:30–33) in the ninth chapter of Romans, Paul states his conclusion about Israel, and by so doing he returns to the great theme of his letter: justification by faith—being made right before God. The Gentiles have achieved right standing before God (9:30) because of their faith, and the Jews have lost it (9:31) because of their lack of faith (9:32). Without success the Jews had tried to earn righteousness based on works, and because of this futile effort, "They have stumbled over the stumbling stone" (ESV).

At this point Paul draws upon one of the New Testament writers' favorite excerpts from the Old Testament as he gives us a combination of Isaiah 8:14 and 28:16 (9:33; see also Mark 12:10–11 and 1 Peter 2:6–8). These verses give us a picture of a stone that can be used in two ways: as an obstacle we can stumble over or as a building block we can use as a firm foundation. It is the same stone in each case. Whether it becomes a help or a hindrance depends upon the response of a person to it.

Similarly, the stone in Paul's illustration can elicit two responses from the one who comes upon it. For the Jews who refused to accept the idea of being made right before God on the basis of faith alone, Jesus Christ was a source of stumbling. On the other hand, for the one who can accept that idea, Christ becomes the firm foundation.

Here then is found another idea that must be held in conjunction with that of the sovereignty of God: the concept of the freedom of the individual person. It is the same Christ that has been confronted by both Jews and Gentiles. Whether He has become a source of stumbling or a building block depends not upon Him but upon their individual willful responses to Him.

The End of the Law

Earlier in chapter 9 Paul shared with his readers his "agony" over Israel's rejection of Jesus Christ. Now he shares his prayer "that they might be saved" (10:1, KJV). He points out that while they are zealous for God, their zeal is uninformed and unenlightened.

And so were the Jews about whom Paul wrote who refused to accept God's righteousness through faith in Jesus Christ. Paul says that they are ignorant of this righteousness (10:2), but from what he has just said in chapter 9, it is a willful ignorance. The old saying is true: no one is so blind as the one who refuses to see; no one is so ignorant as the one who willingly ignores the truth.

Paul is saying that the Jews have failed because they have tried to achieve right standing before God by their own efforts (10:31). They have tried to do it their "own way" through following the Law, but they have failed because "Christ is the culmination of the law" (10:4, NIV). Some Bible teachers have correctly pointed out that the term used here for "culmination" can also mean "goal" or "fulfillment." But Paul seems to be saying more than that. He is saying that Christ is the "end" (ESV), the termination, of the Law as a means of achieving a right relationship with God. Righteousness *now* is available only through faith in Jesus Christ.

There is an important word for us in this part of Paul's teaching. So often in our zeal we want to do God's work in the church "our way." We latch on to some interpretation of the Christian faith as being the *only* way. And in our misplaced zeal we become critical of others because they don't follow *our* rules. Then schisms develop and the spirit of Jesus is completely lost. But Paul is pointing us beyond either the blindness or the arrogance of our way to Jesus Christ, for only through Him do we have a right relationship with God.

The Confession of Faith

Paraphrasing Moses' farewell message to the Israelites before his death (Deuteronomy 30:11–14), Paul applies this Old Testament text to Christ to demonstrate His accessibility (10:6–8). No one has to "ascend into heaven" to bring Christ down, for He has already become the Incarnate One who has lived among us and died for us (10:6). Furthermore, no one has to. "'Who will descend into the abyss?' (that is, to bring Christ up from the dead)" (10:7, NASB), for the resurrection is already accomplished. Christ becomes a very present reality for the person who believes and confesses the word of faith (10:8).

Different church groups today formulate creeds and confessions of faith that define and codify their beliefs. But in verse 9 Paul gives the earliest confession of faith: Jesus is Lord! For Paul, this is a powerful statement of faith because the Greek word he uses for "Lord" is the same word that is used for God in the Old Testament.

In Romans 10:9 Paul has compressed into a few words a revolutionary and life-changing truth: "If you declare with your mouth, 'Jesus is Lord,' and believe in your heart that God raised him from the dead, you will be saved" (NIV). Confession and belief in this verse are parallel to each other. They are not different steps in a "plan of salvation."

You might have heard someone talk about the ABCs of salvation: recognize that All have sinned (3:23), Believe in Jesus (10:9), and Confess Him before others (10:9). Because they are stated in alphabetical order, it's easy to assume that these are chronological steps a person has to take to become a Christian. In this verse, however, the *believing* and *confessing* are synonymous. In fact, the confessing is mentioned before the believing. It is important to understand, though, that you can't have one without the other and be saved. For example, a parrot can be taught the phrase "Jesus is Lord," but reciting it won't make the bird a Christian. The confession with the lips parallels what is believed in the heart, just as "righteousness" and "salvation" are in this next verse: "For with the heart one believes and is justified, and with the mouth one confesses and is saved" (10:10, ESV).

This belief-and-confession is also parallel to calling upon the name of the Lord (10:13). When the Old Testament prophet used the same phrase many years before—"And it will come about that everyone who calls on the name of the LORD will be saved" (Joel 2:32, NASB)—his meaning involved more than merely "calling" on the Lord's name. Rather, it called for complete faithfulness and loyalty to Him. Certainly this is what Paul had in mind here: we profess our allegiance to Christ—which is the same as confessing Him as Lord.

Furthermore, this belief/confession/calling-upon-the-name is the way that everyone is saved. There is no alternative procedure for any special group. Paul makes this clear when he writes, "For there is no distinction between Jew and Greek; for the same Lord is Lord of all, bestowing his riches on all who call on him" (10:12, ESV). Paul's word for us is the same as it was for his readers in the first-century Jewish and Gentile community in Rome: We are not made right before God through any form of sterile legalism. We are made right by believing *in* the Lord.

The Disobedience of Israel

Now Paul raises an important question: Have the Jews really had a fair opportunity to make the kind of believing confession he has just described? After all, a person can't call upon the name of the Lord if he or she has not believed. And a person certainly can't believe without the opportunity of hearing about the Lord. Hearing requires a preacher, and there is no preacher unless one is sent by God (10:14–15).

As a preacher of the Word and as one sent by God, Paul answers the questions and points he has raised by quoting from several Old Testament scriptures.

In verse 16 Paul reminds his readers of Isaiah's words, "Lord, who has believed our message?" (NIV), to show that the Word has been heard, but it has not been believed. The Jews had a long history of hearing without believing. Paul knew then, as we do now, that "hearing" and reciting laws and creeds was not enough—we must act on our belief for it to be genuine.

Paul next draws from the majestic words of Psalm 19 to show that God's creative handiwork in all of our vast universe points to Jesus Christ as the Savior of the world. (Stop a moment and turn to Psalm 19 in your Bible and read the marvelous witness of God's glory as seen around us every day.) Remember, too, that at the time of Paul's writing, the word about Christ had penetrated the known world (10:18).

Finally, Paul used a collection of verses (Deuteronomy 32:21; Isaiah 65:1–2) to answer the objection that the Jews themselves had possibly not understood (10:19–21). But how could they fail to understand? They had received God's special revelation through the Law. Without question, they were the chosen ones who had received historical and religious preparation for the coming of the Christ—the Messiah. They had the background to understand. Yet even the Gentiles, who had enjoyed no such privilege and who had received no such preparation, had understood and had believed when they heard the Good News of salvation through Jesus Christ. From Paul's point of view, the Jews—Israel—had no excuse for not knowing.

How much more are people today without excuse with almost 2,000 years of Christian history and experience behind us? Today we have the advantage of easy accessibility to Scripture, and we live in a culture that is both familiar and comfortable with Christian ideals. Most certainly, if we reject Jesus Christ, it is not because we have lacked opportunity to know about Him.

The Ultimate Triumph of God (11:1–36)

The good word for the Jews, however, is that even though Israel had rejected God, He had not rejected them, and Paul cites himself as an example: "For I also am an Israelite, of the seed of Abraham, of the tribe of Benjamin" (11:1, KJV). The thought here reflects the quotation in 10:21. Although Israel has been a disobedient and contrary people, God has continued to reach out to them. And the fact that the Lord will triumph despite their rejection of Him is the theme of this eleventh chapter in which Paul concludes his discussion of the Jews' rejection of Jesus Christ.

The Faithful Remnant

The truth that God has not rejected Israel—His chosen people, the Jews—is demonstrated for Paul in his own experience. He himself is an Israelite, a descendent of Abraham, and he hasn't been forsaken by God (11:1). In fact, even before his conversion, when he was the archenemy of Christians and of the church, God had still extended His grace toward Paul. Implicit in Paul's reference to himself is the idea that since God didn't reject him in spite of all that he had done, God will not forsake or reject the other Jews either (11:1–6).

Again Paul refers to a well-known Old Testament figure to illustrate his point (11:2–4). When Elijah had complained to God that he was the only one left in Israel who had remained faithful, God responded that there were 7,000 who had "not bowed the knee to the image of Baal" (KJV). Just as there had been a sizable group then who were faithful to God, so Paul implies that the rejection by the Jews now is not total or final. Rather, there is a remnant of Israel who have responded to God in faith in Jesus Christ (11:5). That these have accepted Christ by grace through faith clearly demonstrates that God has not rejected Israel!

Unfaithful Israel

The Jews who responded to God in faith and found salvation are called the "elect," the ones who are chosen (11:7, NIV). The rest, Paul says, have been blinded. Again he goes to the Old Testament (11:8), where he finds this blindness or hardening on the part of Israel referred to in Isaiah 29:10. There God is said to have given the people "eyes that would not see and ears that would not hear" (ESV). A similar phrase is found in Psalm 69:22–23, which Paul also quotes (11:9–10). Paul is careful to quote from the Old Testament scriptures when he wants to get a point across to the Jews.

If taken out of context, these verses might be interpreted to mean that God caused some people to be blinded and, by implication, that He also caused others to see. But we must remember that throughout this entire passage (chapters 9–11), Paul has talked about the freedom of the will and the consequent responsibility of people for accepting or rejecting God. Again we can say with Paul that God is ultimately responsible for the willful blindness of those who reject Him in that He confronted them with a decision that demanded acceptance or rejection. But what we are describing is the *result* of God's action and not His purpose.

God does not confront people in order to force them to reject Him, but when He does confront them, many do reject Him.

The Jealousy of Israel

Is the rejection of God's plan of salvation by the Jews irreversible? Paul never suggests such a possibility. Instead, in these verses he reveals his hope that their rejection may ultimately lead to their acceptance of God's salvation (11:11–16). His argument is as follows: When the Jews rejected the provision of being made right before God through Jesus Christ, salvation was then preached to the Gentiles (11:1). And now, because of this, Paul hopes the Jews will be provoked by jealousy (at seeing others enjoying what could be theirs) and accept this salvation for themselves.

We see in Paul's keen perception of human nature something we can easily recognize today. We've probably all known the feeling of being jealous of someone else's possession—a possession we already had an opportunity to own but chose not to.

After all, Paul insists, if Israel's rejection of God caused something good—the gift of salvation made available to Gentiles—how much more good can their own acceptance of God's plan cause (11:12–15)? Paul seems to be the eternal optimist. And to make his point clear to them, he uses the analogy of "firstfruits" (11:16, ESV). According to Old Testament teaching, the first portion of anything grown or made was to be dedicated to God. Referring then to dough, Paul suggests that if the first part is holy, then the whole "lump"—batch—is holy. And taking the analogy even further, he illustrates the same idea of a part representing the whole by referring to a tree: "If the root is holy, the branches are as well" (11:16, NASB). But Paul is also realistic. He indicates that the jealousy may cause only *some* of the Jews to be saved (11:14). Furthermore, his development of the olive tree analogy that follows suggests that branches can be pruned from the tree.

The Olive Tree

In horticultural procedures of the first century, cultivated olive branches were grafted onto a wild olive trunk to give the branches renewed vitality. To do the opposite, to graft wild branches onto a cultivated trunk, would be unexpected. That is precisely what Paul is saying in his use of the olive tree illustration: God has done the unexpected. He has grafted wild olive branches (Gentiles) into an old, cultivated tree—Israel (11:17–24). Furthermore, old, cultivated branches have been pruned from the trunk (verse 20). There are several points that Paul makes with the analogy.

First, there is a continuity about the people of God. The tree represents the ongoing reality of *true Israel,* which is composed of *Jews* and *Gentiles* alike. New branches do not mean a new tree. We should remember Paul's earlier discussion about Abraham (4:11–12) in which he noted that Abraham is the father of all who believe, whether they are circumcised or not. The righteousness attributed to him is the same as that attributed to everyone who believes in Him who raised Jesus from the dead (4:23–24).

Second, the criterion for grafting and pruning is faith, or lack of it. Gentiles have been grafted into the trunk—the people of God—on the basis of their belief; Jews have been cut away from the trunk because of their unbelief. Grafting and pruning are not arbitrary actions of the nurseryman; such actions are based upon the presence or absence of faith in the branches.

Third, the fact that the Gentiles have been grafted is not to be taken by them as a source of pride (11:18). Paul may be hinting here at some prideful boasting on the part of the Gentiles in the church of Rome. Lest they develop some kind of false pride, Paul reminds them that the roots support the branches and not vice versa.

Fourth, there is a warning in the analogy. Even grafted branches can be pruned (11:21–22). Again Paul warns against a false pride, and he issues a call for faithfulness. Gentiles can be cut off from the tree because of unbelief just as certainly as the Jews were.

Finally, Paul also expresses his hope for the restoration of Israel (11:23–24). The branches that have been pruned because of unbelief can be grafted back through faith.

The Salvation of Israel

Paul introduces the conclusion to his argument as a "mystery" (11:25), as the Greek word is rendered in virtually every English translation. Mystery cults were characteristic of first-century religion in the Roman Empire. Each of these cults emphasized some type of secret knowledge that could be known only by those who were members of that particular group. Paul, however, uses the term "mystery" here and elsewhere to refer to a plan of God, previously hidden but now revealed through Jesus Christ. In other words, a mystery is something that is to be understood (11:1).

What exactly Paul means in explaining this mystery, though, has long been debated by Christian scholars. Paul indicates that a hardening or blindness will afflict part of Israel until the full number of the Gentiles comes in, "and so all Israel shall be saved" (11:26, KJV).

There are two primary ways of interpreting these verses. The first would define Paul's explanation of the "mystery" as simply a continuation of his optimistic hope for Israel stated earlier (11:12, 15). According to this interpretation, Paul stresses that the hardening that has afflicted part of Israel (for indeed some Jews, like him, have not been hardened) serves a purpose. It opens the door for the Gentiles to enter into a saving relationship with God. It is also temporary, for when all of the Gentiles who will be saved have entered, then the heart of the hardened will be melted—Israel, the Jews, will be restored to God.

If one accepts this interpretation, a couple of matters need to be kept in mind. "All Israel" can mean Israel as a whole and not every individual Jew. Support for this idea is found in the *Mishnah*, the written collection of the oral interpretations of the Law that was written around 200 C.E. At one place in this document is found the statement that the whole of Israel would share in the world to come; yet this statement is immediately followed by a list of categories of sinners who would *not* be included. Paul might be thinking of "all Israel" in the same way.

Furthermore, in interpreting the meaning of these verses, we should not forget what Paul has written earlier in the letter. Specifically, he has demonstrated that all human beings are sinners and that all are saved in the same way—by the faith commitment of the *individual person* to the Lordship of Jesus Christ. There is no wholesale conversion of a group or a nation apart from the individual professions of faith of the people within it. So if Paul envisions the salvation of Israel as a whole, he does so on the basis of the commitments of the individual Jews within it. As Paul has said, there is no difference in the way that Jews and Greeks (non-Jews) are saved (10:12). And to suggest there is any other means of salvation is to negate all that Paul has said about justification by faith.

The other primary interpretation involves understanding the two references to Israel in 11:25–26 in different ways. The first ("a part of Israel") would indicate historical Israel; the second ("all Israel") refers to spiritual Israel—everyone who has accepted Christ. Central to this interpretation is the Greek term, which the King James Version and other translations have worded as "so," which can more precisely be translated as "in this way," as the New International Version and English Standard Version render it. The sense of this interpretation could be paraphrased as follows: A hardening and blindness have come upon a part of historical Israel—some of the Jews—which has resulted in the inclusion of Gentiles among God's people. And this conversion of the Gentiles will continue until the full number (all who choose to accept Christ as Savior) are included. It is "in this way," then, that all of spiritual Israel—all of God's people, whether Jews or Gentiles—will be saved.

In favor of this interpretation is Paul's earlier usage of a term more than once and with different meanings in one passage (see "law" in 7:21–23). His discussion of what makes a person a "real Jew" (2:25–29) also indicates that he can conceive of terms like "Jew" and "Israel" to refer to both historical and spiritual realities. This is certainly the case in 9:6–13 where he indicates that not all who are descended from Abraham—that is, Israel—belong to Israel as a national and political entity. For example, Esau and the Edomite nation, which he founded, have never been considered a part of national Israel.

However one interprets the passage, we cannot escape Paul's conclusion that the rejection of God's plan of salvation by the Jews does not defeat His purpose for the world. Whether Jew or Gentile, all people in all time are disobedient, so God offers His mercy to them all (11:32). Even though some may reject God, He triumphs by redeeming those who are receptive to Him! Realizing this ultimate triumph of God, we, too, appreciate and echo Paul's hymn of praise with which he brings this discussion to a close (11:33–36).

＊———————————＊

Lord, thank You for bringing me into Your family. Thank You for the gift of salvation, which makes it possible. AMEN.

So faith comes from hearing, that is, hearing the Good News about Christ.

—Romans 10:17 (NLT)

I had no boyfriend, no friends. I was a big mess. But as I lay there—17, pregnant, and depressed—I thought back to days long ago when I'd attended Sunday school. Words . . . God's Word . . . filtered through my mind, such as "For God so loved the world, that he gave his only begotten Son, that whosoever believeth in him should not perish, but have everlasting life" (John 3:16, KJV).

I thought back to the stories I heard as a child about a God who would never leave me, would never forsake me. Then I prayed the first prayer I'd prayed in years. It wasn't eloquent, but it was real.

"I've really messed up this time, God. If You can do better, please do." That was my moment of change. The moment when heaven met my heart. And God has indeed done better. I had led myself down a dark path, but through God, I had found a silver lining.

I discovered that no matter what I had done in my life, through the forgiveness of Jesus Christ, I was a new creation. I can't say at that moment I realized fully how special I was to God or that I knew then that God had big plans for me. But over time, as I continued to read His Word, I grew in my relationship with Him.

And this path started with the simplest scripture verse of all.

Faith comes when we hear the Good News of Jesus and believe it. We don't need to know the whole Bible well to start our faith journey. We just need to believe and accept what we do know—believe it with all of our hearts. Once I took my life and placed it in Jesus's hands, our relationship grew.

Every relationship has a first step before there is a next step.

—*Tricia Goyer*

Notes

Notes

Notes

LESSON 7: ROMANS 12:1–15:6

Living the Life of Love: Christian Conduct According to Paul

Father, help me understand what Christlike conduct is and how to reflect that conduct in my living. Let my thoughts, words, and actions please and glorify You. AMEN.

"Actions speak louder than words," as the familiar adage says. "Walk the talk" is another way of expressing the same sentiment. Many of us have known people who, with their words, say they know Jesus, all the while living in such a negative or harmful way that it completely negates their spoken testimony. True Christianity has always insisted that there is a vital connection between what we say and the way we act. The teachings of Jesus as well as the writings of the apostles are permeated with reminders that the true measure of a person's faith is not found in what he or she professes as much as it is in his or her lifestyle. Theology and Christian conduct go hand in hand.

Paul certainly saw the link, for his letters are characterized by a balance of reasoned explanation of Christian doctrine and practical advice about Christian living. For him, there was an inseparable bond between belief and behavior.

Nowhere in his writings can this connection be seen more clearly than in this epistle to the Romans. After his eleven-chapter discussion of the essentials of Christian doctrine, he turns in chapter 12 to admonitions about Christian living. The word *therefore* in 12:1 is crucial for seeing the relationship between what follows and what has gone before. By that one word, Paul effectively says, "Because all of this (chapters 1–11) is true, here then is how we should live."

The Foundation of Christian Conduct (12:1–2)

Before dealing with specific examples of Christian conduct, Paul first states a principle that guides all action: Christians are to present their total being—the sum total of their existence—to God as an act of worship (12:1).

We have seen earlier in our study that Paul's Hebrew understanding of the nature of humankind does not allow a division of life into different, separate compartments. Spirit, body, mind, and heart are just different ways of looking at the same reality—the total self or soul. For this reason, Paul's appeal for the dedication of the body is a call for the total commitment of the self.

The analogy that Paul uses is that of sacrificial worship, familiar to first-century Jews and non-Jews alike. The Christians are admonished to present their bodies as a "living sacrifice" (12:1), in contrast to the Old Testament practice of offering dead animals. In their devotion, Christians are to continually give their lives to God. Paul encourages his readers throughout all time to give the gift that keeps on giving! "Reasonable service" (KJV) can also be translated as "spiritual worship" (ESV).

As opposed to the external rituals often associated with the practice of religion, the continuing gift of a life dedicated to God is true inner, spiritual worship.

"When in Rome, do as the Romans do" is a familiar word of advice still frequently given about accommodating to one's surroundings. But that is just the opposite of what Paul says to his readers here. They are in Rome, and he reminds them that they should *not* do as their fellow Romans are doing.

We all face the glaring temptation, even as Christians, to conform to the culture and standards of the society in which we live. It is easy to "go with the flow" of modern life and avoid making ripples, but that is precisely what Paul is warning against here.

In colorful language, Paul is telling his readers that rather than conforming to the standards of the world about them, they should be transformed by the renewing of their minds—their total selves (12:2). The word *transform* Paul uses here is the same word used of Jesus when He was transfigured. From this we learn that as Christians we are to live a life that has been radically and totally changed by encounter with Jesus Christ. Such a transformation enables the Christian believer to "discern what is the will of God, what is good and acceptable and perfect" (verse 2, ESV). To Paul, the will of God was not a mystery but a reality.

The Context of Christian Conduct: The Body of Christ (12:3–8)

Many word pictures are used by Paul to depict the church. He uses phrases that describe it as the people or family of God. He calls it God's temple and the bride of Christ. No image does he develop more completely, however, than that of the body of Christ. Found also in 1 Corinthians 12:12–27, Ephesians 1:22–23, and Colossians 1:18–24, this metaphor is particularly apt here for understanding Christian behavior.

Two key ideas are bound up within this metaphor: unity and diversity. Unity or oneness defines both the relationship of the believer with Christ and the relationship of the believer with other Christians. Diversity, on the other hand, is specifically descriptive of our relationship as Christians with other Christians.

Oneness with Christ has been alluded to many times in Romans, particularly in Paul's use of the phrase *in Christ.* When we accept God's grace as offered in Jesus Christ, we enter into a relationship with the Godhead that is so intimate and personal that it is best defined as a "union." There is a mutual indwelling of Christ and the Christian: He lives in the believer, and the believer lives in Him. Oneness with Christ, that *vertical* dimension of the Christian experience, is not the only feeling of unity realized within the body of Christ. There is also the *horizontal* dimension of oneness with fellow Christians. This common bond unites each person to the other just as each is bound to Christ. This means then that what affects anyone in the body of Christ affects everyone else.

Just as there is unity between Christians, there is also a healthy diversity. A human body is composed of different limbs and organs that have quite distinctive functions. The foot walks, the eye sees, and the stomach digests. The function of each part, though, contributes to the good of the whole body. No part of the body exists only for itself; no function of the body is performed for the sake of only one part. Paul's analogy then is easily applied to the church. No individual Christian exists or functions only for himself. Each is related to other Christians who have different gifts and abilities, but all function for the good of the whole (12:4–5).

Consequently, each member of the church should not think of themselves more highly than they ought (verse 3). There is nothing wrong with healthy self-esteem, but there is a problem with an inflated view of one's own worth. We've all had the sad experience of knowing conceited people who have an unrealistic estimate of their own importance. In an attempt to magnify their own worth, they constantly undercut and belittle everyone else. Those who suffer from overextended egos usually exalt themselves at the expense of others.

As we shall see in chapter 14, a problem of spiritual pride did exist within the church at Rome. Some members considered themselves to be superior to others in their Christian understanding. Before giving specific advice about that particular problem, Paul spells out here the underlying principle that will serve as a basis for the counsel he will give later.

Seven gifts of the Spirit are listed in verses 6–8. Prophecy refers to inspired preaching, while service probably refers to some type of social service. Those who instruct others in the faith have the gift of teaching. Exhortation (translated in the New International Version as encouragement) is perhaps similar to what we know today as pastoral counseling or simply offering uplifting or inspiring words, and leadership for those who have administrative ability. Both giving and mercy seem to indicate an outreach to the needy.

A comparison of these gifts of the Spirit with those listed in 1 Corinthians 12:4–11 and Ephesians 4:11 reveals some differences. Evidently, Paul does not intend the lists, either individually or collectively, to be exhaustive. Instead, they are *representative* of the gifts that God has bestowed upon individual Christians for the building up of the entire body of Christ.

It is interesting to note that the Greek word translated gifts is the term from which the English word "charismatic" is derived. To apply this word to only one branch of the Christian church, as we often do, is inconsistent with Paul's understanding. For him, all Christians are charismatic, for each has been given a gift from the Holy Spirit.

Inherent in Paul's analogy of the body is his understanding of the worth of the individual before God. By bestowing different gifts on different persons, God demonstrates that we are not to be carbon copies of each other. Each of us is unique. At the same time, though, individuality does not indicate independence. The Christian's full potential as a unique person before God is realized only *in the body*, in relationship to other Christians.

The Content of Christian Conduct: Specific Examples (12:9–15:6)

After setting forth the underlying assumptions upon which his principles for living are based, Paul now turns to some specific examples of Christian conduct in practice. We need to understand, however, that Paul is not trying to formulate a list of rules that a Christian has to follow. That would be legalism, from which he insists that we, as Christians, have been set free. Rather, Paul is giving us instruction by way of concrete examples. He has not tried to be exhaustive, suggesting a Christian response to every situation that a believer might encounter. Again, his examples are representative, "for instance" principles. To be sure, things he had heard about the church in Rome may have influenced his choice of topics, but his discussion is not intended to be comprehensive. These are examples of the way we put our belief into practice.

In Relation to Fellow Christians

Love is one of the most overworked words in the English language. We can use it to mean a variety of sentiments. "I love hot dogs." "I love reading." "I love my cat." "I love my daughter." "I love sailing." "I love God." This overuse tends to confuse the meaning of the word.

Paul's term in 12:9, though, is very explicit, for he uses the word *agape* (uh-GAH-peh), that infrequently used word in the Greek language that came to be used almost exclusively as a Christian term. It means a love that is selfless and self-giving. Devoid of romantic or purely emotional overtones, it is an intentional, volitional love that seeks the best for the other person.

Agape is the kind of love that God has for people. In fact, with the exception of 8:28, where the verb form is used to speak of a person's love for God, the term has been used so far in Romans only to describe divine love. However, Paul uses it here to refer to Christians' love for one another. He is saying that we are to love with the same kind of love that God has given to us.

It is interesting that Paul's great "love" chapter, 1 Corinthians 13, comes amid his discussion of spiritual gifts. And his admonition here in Romans is found in the same context. Love is the superior gift!

Paul urges his readers to let their love be genuine (12:9). No counterfeit substitute is to be allowed. It is quite likely that Paul is thinking about a particular situation in the Roman church. Is it possible that the "strong" and the "weak" (chapter 14) are "putting on a show" when they affirm their love for one another? We don't know for sure, but Paul presses his point home, and we see that in our fellow church members—in fact, in our relations with all of our fellow human beings—love is the crucial virtue.

Next Paul refers to "brotherly love" (12:10, KJV, NASB)—another kind of love, that of a family member for another. Because it follows so quickly the mention of agape in the previous verse, it is possible that the love first mentioned (12:9) is to be directed to all humankind, while the reference in 12:10 is to our relationship with our fellow Christians. In this context, however, it would not be unlikely that Paul might stress this virtue by using more than one expression of love.

An alternate way of translating "Honor one another above yourselves" (12:10, NIV) is "Outdo one other in showing honor," which is how the English Standard Version phrases it. Again, this is the probable meaning in light of the tensions between the "strong" and the "weak." This is certainly appropriate advice for those who try to "outdo" each other by being pushy and self-assertive.

Paul next turns to some pretty practical instruction for his readers in first-century Rome and to those of us who are living in the twenty-first century (12:11–12). We are to reflect Christ to those around us by always taking good care of our affairs. Being a Christian is no excuse for being sloppy or careless in our business affairs. Then, building on this idea, Paul says that the Christian is to be "fervent in spirit"—full of zeal. We are to be excited about our Christian walk. Life "in Christ" is not a casual affair—it demands the full use of our time and energy.

In verse 12 Paul goes on to tell us we are to be full of hope, "persevering in tribulation, devoted" (NASB) or "constant" (ESV) in prayer. There is no room for pessimism, for spreading gloom, even when times may be hard. And we are to be people of prayer, for that is the only way our hope can be sustained and we can cope with the problems of life.

Since Paul is on his way to deliver the collection he has taken among the churches for the poor among the "saints" in Jerusalem, his next instructions are timely (12:13). When we remember that the "saints" (KJV) are living Christians, "the Lord's people" (NIV), the reminder is also important for us. We, too, need to be encouraged to contribute to the needs of the less fortunate people *within* as well as *outside* the church.

Paul's constant concern for the poor in Jerusalem models for us a present-day responsibility for the poor and the hungry in our towns and cities as well as for the starving in underprivileged and Third World countries. No matter how we rationalize the inequality involved in the handling and use of our God-given resources, we can't escape the cry of our brothers and sisters in desperate need.

In Relation to Our Enemies

Paul now closes this twelfth chapter with words of advice
that seem to suggest Christian responses that should be
made to those who are hostile toward Christian believers
(12:14–21). In several places, Paul's words echo the teachings
of Jesus, particularly those given in the Sermon on the Mount
(Matthew 5–7). It can be argued that the overall theme of
these verses in Romans is best summed up in these words:
"Do not be overcome by evil, but overcome evil with good"
(12:21, NASB). Paul is telling us in this part of our scripture
lesson that we are not to retaliate (12:17), we are not to take
revenge (12:19), and we are not even to lash out and condemn those who persecute us in any way. When evil meth-
ods are used to fight evil forces, evil becomes the winner. In
other words, the Christian who has been "transformed by the
renewing of [the] mind" (12:2, KJV) must not stoop to the
tactics of those whose minds have not been renewed.

Next, Paul's encouragement to "rejoice with those who
rejoice; mourn with those who mourn" (12:15, NIV) is often
applied to our relationships within the church. From experience, we can affirm the interpretations of some of the church
fathers who suggested that even with our fellow Christians
the "mourning" is easier than the "rejoicing." It is ironic, but
most of the time we find it easier to empathize with a fellow
Christian who is going through a difficult time or has suffered
bereavement than to rejoice over someone else's success. So
often when another person is experiencing success we are
inclined to ask, "Why is she so fortunate?" "Why doesn't
something like this ever happen to me?" "What has he done

to deserve that?" To applaud someone else's success, to be genuinely happy over the achievements of others, is practical Christianity at work in our relationships with one another.

Within the framework of Paul's discussion in this part of our lesson, this fifteenth verse also gives us guidance for our relationships with non-Christians and even with those who may vigorously oppose our Christian way of life. Weeping and rejoicing with those who are hostile to us are also ways of overcoming evil with good. This is agape in action: wanting the best for others no matter who they may be.

When Paul cautioned his readers to "not be haughty in mind" (12:16, NASB), he was warning them against any form of spiritual arrogance and pride. Arrogance is never more distasteful than when it has a religious label. Paul, the former Pharisee, probably knew so well just how religious people can look with disdain upon the "lowly." It is safe to say that many non-Christians have been turned away from the church because of some who by their actions and reactions have suggested that they and their opinions are better than everyone else's.

Paul is extremely practical in his teaching here as he urges his readers and us to, "so far as it depends on you, be at peace with all people" (12:18, NASB), and to respond to others with genuine love. And once again he points out the "high road" in Christian conduct when he says, "If your enemy is hungry, feed him; if he is thirsty, give him something to drink" (12:20, ESV). These words taken from Proverbs 25:21–22 tell us to respond in love even to those who oppose us and are hostile to us. Then Paul teaches that by acting in this Christlike way we "will heap burning coals on [their] head" (verse 20, ESV).

In saying this, though, I don't believe Paul is suggesting that the motive for such behavior is to make our "enemies" suffer or be embarrassed or uncomfortable—that wouldn't be agape. Rather, for Paul the "burning coals" represent some type of repentance. Love will bring more people to repentance than will retaliation and revenge. As the old adage tells us, "You can attract more flies with honey than you can with vinegar." Again, the key to understanding Paul's teaching here is found in the last verse (12:21): The vicious cycle of evil will only be broken by self-giving love—a love that wills affirmation and good for the other person.

In Relation to the State

For the believers living in Rome, the capital of the sprawling Roman Empire, these words about the Christian's responsibility to the state and the civil authorities are particularly appropriate (13:1–7). During this time, the state was not the enemy of the church, but the potential was there. Just a few years before, Claudius, the emperor, had exiled Jews (some historians think Jewish Christians) from Rome because of suspected sedition. Paul's tentmaking compatriots Aquila and Priscilla were among that group (Acts 18:1). And now at the beginning of Nero's reign, those who had been exiled were returning home. What was to be their attitude toward the government?

Paul urges them to be good citizens who support the government, even with paying their taxes (13:7–8). And because he believes in the absolute sovereignty of God, Paul also believes that government exists to fulfill God's purpose (13:1–2). In fact, he reminds them, the rulers' authority to govern is derived from God Himself. As God's agents, then, rulers exist to punish the evildoer (13:4), not to harm the one who does good (13:3).

Of course, a little later the Roman Empire did become the enemy of the church and persecuted the Christians. During those dark days of persecution, the civil government demanded both loyalty and a worship that belonged to God alone. But for Paul, if government functioned as it should, with responsible use of its derived authority, it and its rulers should be respected and supported. Because of the renewing of our minds (12:2), every aspect of life must reflect our Christian position. Conscience (13:5) requires responsible citizenship.

In Relation to One's Neighbor

This section of Paul's letter (13:8–10) is much like a musical work with a main theme that is then repeated and developed with variations as the piece progresses. The discussion often moves forward by going back and picking up a word or a theme that has already been stated. In 13:8, for example, Paul returns to and restates the theme of agape—selfless love. Here, though, there is an interesting variation.

Paul has just stated in the preceding paragraph that the Christian citizen is to fulfill all his obligations to the state. He is to give what is owed—taxes, revenue, respect, or honor—to those to whom it is due (13:7).

Following up on the idea of debt or obligation, he suggests here that all debts should be paid—with one exception. There is one debt that cannot be paid off, one obligation that can never be completed: the love that is owed to one's fellow human beings. His statement is emphatic: "except the continuing debt to love one another, for whoever loves others has fulfilled the law" (13:8, NIV). It is interesting and significant that Paul doesn't say here that in loving our neighbor, whether across the street or across the world, we are obeying the Law. Instead, he says we have *fulfilled* the Law. Love that has "fulfilled the law" in no way harms or assaults the person or integrity of our neighbor. And to underscore his point, Paul quotes again from the Old Testament scriptures, "You shall love your neighbor as yourself" (Leviticus 19:18, ESV). Once again, Paul emphasizes the truth that the intention of the Law is fulfilled in love (13:10).

The Urgency of the Hour

Inserted at this point in the discussion of Christian conduct is a paragraph that at first glance seems out of place (13:11–14). Unlike the rest of chapters 12–14, it does not suggest a particular ethical response to a specific situation. Yet it does fit. Paul is giving us an added incentive for the kind of behavior that he has been describing throughout chapters 12 and 13: "The day is almost here" (NIV).

Like other Christians of the first century, Paul lived each day with an attitude of expectancy. His earlier writings indicate that he anticipated being alive at the time of Christ's return (1 Thessalonians 4:17, for example). Evidently he still had that anticipation as he wrote the epistle to the Romans, for he reminds his readers that "the hour has already come" (13:11, NIV) and that "the day is at hand" (13:12, NIV).

Particularly important is the clause "salvation is nearer to us now than when we first believed" (13:11, ESV). Two significant ideas are intertwined here. First is the idea that salvation is a process with past, present, and future dimensions. Paul can write of it as past experience, present reality, and future hope. In these verses the emphasis is future; salvation is the goal toward which we move, and that will not be completed until "that day," the ultimate triumph of Christ in His Second Coming. So often we Christians tend to concentrate on a past event when we think about salvation instead of realizing that the process is going on at the present and that it will be completed in the future.

The second idea in these words from 13:11 is that Paul and his readers were keenly aware of the shortness of time because of their belief that the Second Coming of Christ could occur at any moment. This, of course, accounts for his feeling of urgency for living constantly in a way acceptable to God, and in a way that will point others to their need for Jesus Christ.

Even today many well-intentioned Christians concentrate almost exclusively on the return of Christ. It is true that the Second Coming of Jesus completes God's plan of salvation for the world, but we must avoid becoming so preoccupied with this event that how we live here and now becomes secondary, or as Oliver Wendell Holmes Sr. is credited with saying, "Some people are so heavenly minded that they are of no earthly good." While he anticipated Christ's return, Paul also saw it as reason for living a holy life here and now—one in which we walk honestly, avoiding the sins mentioned in verse 13, and live in relationship with others as described throughout this entire lesson.

In Relationship to Weaker Christians

Paul's examples of Christian conduct so far have been quite general. Virtually all of the instructions that he has shared with his readers and with us deal with those situations that could be confronted by any first-century Christian and church. Within these general instructions on Christian behavior, however, there have been a few statements that possibly point directly to the situation in the church at Rome about which Paul had heard. Now, though, the general instructions give way to advice about a specific situation that is confronting the Roman congregations (14:1–15:6).

The particular problem confronting the church was the presence of two distinct groups who were at odds with each other: the "strong" and the "weak." Although the identities of the two are not spelled out by Paul, the consensus of commentators seems to be that the "weak" are the Jewish Christians, and the "strong" are those who have come into the church from a Gentile background.

The "weak" have scruples about eating meat and drinking wine (14:2, 21), and they have a particular regard for one day (most likely the Sabbath) over the others (14:5–6). The "strong," on the other hand, are not bothered by such matters, for they correctly feel that their faith has freed them from the strictures of diet and calendar. It seems apparent that the "strong" group is in the majority, and it is with them that Paul identifies (15:1).

Although both groups are contributing to the disharmony in the church, most of Paul's suggestions seem to be directed to the "strong." As the majority group, they must shoulder most of the responsibility in trying to restore the unity that Paul feels is so essential.

Disunity was not an uncommon problem in first-century churches. For example, Philippi, a predominantly Gentile congregation, experienced such serious strife that Paul, in writing to them, even called some of the disagreeing people by name in an effort to restore their sense of oneness (Philippians 4:2). In the Corinthian church at least four factions existed, and each claimed a different leader (1 Corinthians 1:10 and following)! Since two of these groups pledged loyalty to Peter and Paul, names associated with Jewish and with Gentile Christianity, respectively, it is possible that at least part of the problem in Corinth was the same as the problem that confronted the church in Rome, which was the challenge of creating one united group of *Christians* out of *Jews* and *Gentiles* who knew Christ as their Lord and Savior. Finally, we should not forget that even as Paul was writing these words, he was preparing for his trip to Jerusalem to try to cement a bond between Jewish and Gentile Christians.

Even before we get into the details of Paul's counsel in meeting this crisis, there are two conclusions that we can draw that have a practical application to the divisions confronting Christians today.

First, the very fact that divisions and tensions exist is evidence that Christians are not perfect. Perfection, complete salvation, is the goal toward which we move, but we have not arrived there yet! Paul's advice to the Roman Christians then was to be "transformed by the renewing of your mind" (12:2, KJV), and this most certainly is a sound word for us today.

Second, when divisions occur, it is the "strong" group that should assume the responsibility for restoring unity.

Central to Paul's understanding of the proper way to eliminate the discord is the idea of acceptance. "As for the one who is weak in faith, welcome him, but not to quarrel over opinions" (14:1, ESV), and "Whoever thus serves Christ is acceptable to God" (verse 18, ESV). Each group must accept the other, even as they have been accepted by Christ.

Paul then makes it clear that neither of these two groups is to pass judgment on the other (14:3, 13). Both are to follow their convictions, but each is to understand that both groups have the same motivation: to honor God (14:5–6). Their goals are the same; it is in the means of achieving those goals that they differ. Consequently, neither is to force their convictions on the other.

At this point, particular advice is given to the "strong" (14:13–23). When it came to the dietary regulations—the kind of food they ate—Paul readily agreed that these were no longer binding upon the Christian (14:14; Mark 7:19). Such rules are part of the Jewish law from which the Christian has been set free. At the same time, though, this freedom should not become a source of arrogance or pride. Instead, the feelings and beliefs of those Christians who held to the Jewish food laws should be respected, for if they were persuaded to do something that violated their conscience, they were being encouraged to sin (14:14, 23). Rather than flaunting their freedom, the "strong" should also be free and mature, doing nothing that would cause confusion, stumbling, or injury to the weaker Christian (14:13, 15, 21). The one-word summary of Christian behavior is not freedom but love.

In this matter of Christian responsibility, the Christian's pattern of life can be compared to a tightrope walker. The success of the walk depends on maintaining a careful balance. The Christian must "walk the fine line" that separates the right to live according to the dictates of one's conscience and the responsibility not to offend a weaker brother or sister.

But there is also another tension, another tightrope effect, that confronts the reader in this discussion. It is one that is suggested by Paul's call for unity. How do we remain true to our convictions and yet maintain harmony with those who don't see things as we do? Should unity among Christians be maintained at all costs, even at the cost of compromising convictions? Or should we remain true to our conscience at the expense of Christian harmony?

These are delicate questions for which there are no easy answers. But Paul does suggest some guidelines here. Acceptance of those with differing opinions, tolerance for their opinions, and respect for the motivation behind those opinions will go a long way in helping opposing groups to pursue "what leads to peace and to mutual edification" (14:19, NIV). If all of this is done in the spirit of love that seeks the best for the other person or group (15:2)—the love exemplified in Christ Jesus (15:3)—then the harmony, accord, and unity for which Paul prays for his readers (15:5–6) may yet become a reality in the church today.

Jesus, You are concerned not only with what I say and what I do but also with who I am. As I seek to give all of myself to You, give me all I need to be like You. AMEN.

But as for you, why do you judge your brother or sister? Or you as well, why do you regard your brother or sister with contempt? For we will all appear before the judgment seat of God.

—Romans 14:10 (NASB)

Recently I was on the receiving end of a snap judgment. A woman sent a hurtful email accusing me of something I didn't do. It made me feel like she'd beaten me with a baseball bat, especially because I was innocent and she had no right to say such things to me. It took three pots of tea and the advice of a good friend for me before I could respond graciously to her.

We all know it's wrong to make snap judgments about people or to condemn them without getting the full story. We know it's not what Jesus would want us to do. We know that when we do it, it could be that we're being ignorant of the story behind the person's actions. The other person may have a really good motivation for being a certain way or doing certain things.

Granted, sometimes we make a snap judgment and we're right, but how often does that happen? And the times we're wrong usually cause more damage than it's worth, so we know we shouldn't make snap judgments. We should give people the benefit of the doubt, and we should be patient and considerate to others, giving them a chance to explain themselves.

We know all this in our heads, but we still make snap judgments anyway. It's almost automatic. I'm hoping this experience will make me rethink the next time I might make a snap judgment against someone else. I want to remember how hurt I felt so that I'll hesitate before doing something that might make someone else feel the way I did.

—*Camy Tang*

Notes

Notes

Notes

The Imitation of Christ and the Obedience of Faith

Lord, as You said in Your Word, "obedience is better than sacrifice." Let what I learn in this lesson stir me to obey You more. AMEN.

"The proof of the pudding is in the eating," said the father as he and his son pushed the handmade sailboat into the water. The saying was new to the boy, and quite understandably he saw no relationship between pudding and boats and said so. The father then explained what he meant by using the old expression: No matter how detailed their plans and how skilled their craftsmanship, the real test for the boat was its ability to sail. If it couldn't, their work would fail.

To some extent that same saying can be applied to Paul's discussion of Christian doctrine and his advice about Christian living that is found in the epistle to the Romans. Does it work? The real test is found in the kind of life lived by a person who tries it.

The last two chapters of Romans might be considered by some people to be insignificant in comparison to all that has been studied before. Most of what remains consists of travel plans and personal greetings. But what we will study in this lesson is profoundly important, for here is the "proof of the pudding."

In these chapters, we get a glimpse of the personal life of the writer of this epistle—the Apostle Paul. Now we will see how he applied what he believed and preached to life. It is true that Paul didn't write these words for that purpose; they were intended to tell his travel plans and to give his personal greetings. But throughout all of this, we see the love and the concern of a person who has experienced justification by faith and whose plans are motivated by the desire to share that faith and all its implications with others.

Christ's Acceptance of Both Jews and Non-Jews

Everyone learns by imitation. Children mimic what they see, and if they have good examples to follow, they learn acceptable behavior. Earlier in this letter to the Romans (8:14–17), Paul has identified Christians as *children* of God; now he points to the One they are to imitate: Jesus Christ.

In His Steps by Charles M. Sheldon is one of the most popular religious books ever published. Since its first release in 1896 it is estimated that more than 50 million copies have been sold. This fascinating story speaks to the question "What would Jesus do?" in the complicated circumstances that face people in the give-and-take of daily living. When confronted one day by a person in desperate need, the central character of the story, Dr. Henry Maxwell, asked himself, *What would Jesus do in this situation if He were me?* This became the central question of his life, and as the story unfolds, we catch a dramatic glimpse of what God will do with people and a church committed to a practical expression of the Christian faith.

Of course, it isn't possible for us to do *exactly* what Jesus would do in every situation. As the Son of God, His words and actions were flawless. And we so often fall short of God's best for us. But our calling as Christians is to be imitators of Christ.

Paul suggests two ideas in this part of our lesson (15:7–13) that can be imitated by the believer. The first is *acceptance*. Speaking to both opposing groups in the church at Rome—Gentiles and Jews—he writes, "Accept one another, just as Christ also accepted us, for the glory of God" (15:7, NASB). The model Paul gives us here for accepting each other is the impartial Christ who included all people everywhere in His salvation plan—even the two groups in the Roman church. This verse makes it clear that God is glorified when Christians accept each other and live in unity and harmony with one another even though they have differences.

The second idea that Paul suggests we should imitate is "servanthood." The Greek word translated as "servant" in most versions of the Bible is the word from which we derive our English word *deacon*. Although in this verse Paul does not specifically encourage his readers to imitate Christ's servanthood, the idea is clearly stated in Philippians 2:5–11. But it is also implicit in what Paul is saying here. Christ as "Servant" is the embodiment of the agape love that Paul sees as the heart of all Christian behavior.

Paul amplifies this truth when he writes that Christ has become a servant to "the circumcision" (15:8, NASB, KJV).

He is referring to "the Jews" (verse 8, NIV). In becoming a servant to the Jewish people, Jesus Christ confirmed and fulfilled the promises God had made centuries before to the Old Testament patriarchs. Paul wanted his readers to see that because Jesus Christ came for the Jews, they are to praise and glorify Him because He kept His word.

Then Paul moves on to enlarge his point by relating verse 9 to the wording in verse 8: The non-Jews—Gentiles—"might glorify God for his mercy" (NIV) through the coming of Jesus Christ. In other words, both Jew and non-Jew alike can unite in praising God for the saving work of Jesus Christ on Calvary.

Finally, Paul clinches his argument that non-Jews have always been a part of God's eternal plan by giving his readers four quotes from the Old Testament (Deuteronomy 32:43; Psalms 18:49 and 117:1; and Isaiah 11:10). Each of these refers to the Gentiles as those who praise and hope in God (15:9–12).

Paul's model for inclusiveness is clear. Even as Jesus Christ came to save both Jews and non-Jews in spite of their differences, so they as a church are to include everyone who accepts Jesus Christ. The specific disagreements that threaten to divide Christians and churches today may differ greatly from what plagued the Roman Christians, but Paul's message to them applies equally well to us.

Paul now closes out this part of our lesson by offering another prayer of blessing for his readers (15:13). Earlier he prayed, "Now the God of patience and consolation grant you to be likeminded one toward another . . ." (15:5, KJV). This time he prays, "May the God of hope fill you with all joy and peace as you trust in him, so that you may overflow with hope by the power of the Holy Spirit" (NIV). Because of the way the Greek is written, the idea expressed here may be that God is the source of hope, or it may mean that God is the object of hope. Perhaps Paul means both. Or perhaps rather than being ambiguous, he is intentionally suggesting both that hope has its origin in God and that God is the only true object of hope. For hope that is not founded in God is not hope at all.

Paul's prayer is that the Roman Christians, through the power of the Holy Spirit, may abound in hope, for it is only through a living hope in God that they, and we, can find joy and peace.

Paul's Ministry to the Gentiles

Paul (15:14–24) now returns to the subject with which he began this epistle: his plans to visit the church at Rome and his reasons for writing these words (see 1:8–15). Included in this discussion are Paul's autobiographical observations about his ministry to the Gentiles. Since he has just encouraged the mutual acceptance of Jew and Greek—non-Jew—within the church because of Christ's acceptance of them both (15:7), his comments here are particularly relevant. Without any indication of boasting that he has "practiced what he preaches," these words reveal his own personal pilgrimage as a Jew in accepting non-Jews within the fellowship of the believers.

By way of introduction to this line of thinking, Paul tactfully compliments his readers for their maturity in faith. Despite their differences, he is convinced that they are filled with goodness and knowledge, and they are able to teach one another about the Christian life (15:14).

How wonderfully thoughtful Paul is as he affirms these Roman Christians. There is an important lesson in this model this wise apostle has given us. We live in a world of conflicting ideologies and frightful pressures. Alienation and loneliness are diseases of our time. Terrorism and threats of war, economic uncertainty, and imbalance of resources are ongoing threats. But as Christians whose present and future are grounded in the Good News of Jesus Christ, our hope is in God. Together we can be agents of change under the power of the Holy Spirit. And when we affirm each other as Christian brothers and sisters despite our differences, God will use us to influence our neighbors for Christ.

Incidentally, when Paul compliments the Roman Christians for their knowledge, his reference is not to their education but to their thorough understanding of the gospel. This is a strong affirmation of their faith, for they had attained a remarkable level of Christian maturity without the assistance of an apostle.

But at the same time, Paul knows that even quite mature Christians need reminders. The call to "remember" is found frequently throughout the Old Testament. And "remembrance" stands at the heart of the worship of the church. The Lord's Supper, for example, was instituted as a way of remembering; when we celebrate it, we are reminded once again of the love of God and the sacrifice of Jesus Christ. Paul says here that he has written boldly, not because the Roman Christians aren't informed but by way of reminder (15:15).

The word *reminder* is significant for another reason as well. As you will recall from the introduction to this epistle, we saw that Paul was writing to a church that he had neither founded nor visited. However, it was a church that shared his faith in Jesus Christ. Such being the case, he does not think of himself as telling them anything new. What he writes out of his heartfelt convictions is a reminder of the gospel that they and he share.

In this part of our lesson, as Paul begins to bring his letter to a close, we catch some interesting insights into the person and heart of this great Christian. He seems to want them to understand him as he says he has written forthrightly and boldly because of his responsibility to them as a minister to the non-Jews. And the majority of the Christians in the church at Rome were from a Gentile background. As apostle to the Gentiles, then, Paul sees them as among those whom he has been called to serve (15:15–16).

An intriguing picture of the role of a minister is found in verse 16. Drawing an analogy from Jewish worship, Paul suggests that as a minister, he functions as a priest before God. One of the responsibilities of the Jewish priests was to make the sacrifices and present the offerings of the people to God. How does that apply to Paul, and what kind of an offering does Paul make? To complete the picture, Paul sees the Gentile Christians as his offering, and his prayer is that his life's work, the Gentile church, may be an acceptable offering to God.

At a later time Paul suggests that the Christian should strive to be "a worker who does not need to be ashamed" (2 Timothy 2:15, NASB). Here now, as he reflects upon his ministry to the Gentiles, Paul indicates that he is proud of his work for God (Romans 15:17). But as the next verse indicates, his pride is not in what *he* has accomplished but in what Christ has accomplished in him (15:18).

At times Paul shares with his readers what God had done *for* him (see Galatians 1:13 and following). Here, though, he tells of what God has done *through* him. Many people, in reading Paul's writings, get the impression that he had an inflated ego. But that is not the case. Though he begins by saying, "In Christ Jesus, then, I have reason to be proud of my work for God," he goes on to add, "For I will not venture to speak of anything except what Christ has accomplished through me" (15:17–18, ESV).

Next, in just a few words, Paul bears witness to what Christ has done through him, "by the power of signs and wonders, by the power of the Spirit of God—so that from Jerusalem and all the way around to Illyricum I have fulfilled the ministry of the gospel of Christ" (15:19, ESV). The book of Acts doesn't mention a missionary visit to Illyricum (covering parts of what is now Albania, Kosovo, Montenegro, Serbia, Bosnia and Herzegovina, Croatia, and Slovenia), but neither does it seem likely that we have a complete record of Paul's extensive travels over so many years. Another of Paul's epistles, 2 Corinthians 11:23, seems to indicate this.

As was stated in the introduction to these lessons, Paul next identifies what he believed was his special call: "It has always been my ambition to preach the gospel where Christ was not known, so that I would not be building on someone else's foundation" (15:20, NIV). This, in part, explains the wide geographical circle he traveled in his missionary journeys. And in support of this call, he quotes in 15:21 the prophetic words from Isaiah 52:15: "For what they were not told, they will see, and what they have not heard, they will understand" (NIV).

Now that Paul's work in the Aegean Basin was almost complete, he turned his attention to the future and spoke of his passion to move on to Spain (15:23–24). Of course, Paul doesn't mean that there wasn't any more work to be done in that area. Although Christianity was now firmly established in these areas, leadership was still needed for the young but maturing churches. But Paul knows that others can provide this nurturing ministry. For him, the burning desire was to start west toward Spain as soon as possible, and in so doing the gospel would then penetrate to the far western boundaries of the Roman Empire.

Travel to Spain would also give Paul the opportunity to stop off on the way and visit Rome, something he had wanted to do for so long (1:13). He expresses the feeling, though, that his visit to Rome will not be purely social. He has already expressed the expectation that both he and they will be mutually encouraged and blessed by spending some time together (1:11–12). And, of course, he hopes in such a visit to win converts there as he has in other Gentile centers (1:13). Also, Paul is hoping that his visit will encourage them to assist him in his journey to Spain. His words "to be helped on my way there by you" (15:24, NASB) seem to be a request for their financial assistance as he undertakes his mission to Spain.

Paul's Ministry to the Jewish Christians

As we have already seen, though, financial support is not all that Paul hopes to receive from the Roman Christians. In this long letter, he has taught them much about what it means to be followers of Christ, and he has urged them to be inclusive in their faith, to be accepting of each other, and to live in unity as people who have accepted the grace that God has offered in Jesus. And he has called on them for prayer support as he moves steadfastly forward in his effort to promote unity in the church as a whole.

Paul next informs his readers that before he can visit them or travel on to Spain, he must first make a trip back to Jerusalem (15:25–33). Influenced by Paul, Gentile churches in Macedonia and Achaia (Greece) have collected money for the impoverished Jewish Christians in Jerusalem, and he intends to deliver it personally. It is his hope that the offering and the love behind it will cement a bond between the Jewish and non-Jewish Christians based on their mutual recognition of their need for each other. Paul continues to be grieved by a divided church! And he feels that anything he can do to overcome that division, even if it delays his plans, must be done. As much as he wants to go to Rome and then on to Spain, his trip to Jerusalem has first priority.

In these closing verses of this fifteenth chapter, Paul continues to share his deepest feelings with his Christian friends in Rome. He knows there is no guarantee that his gift of money from the Gentile Christians will be accepted by the believers in Jerusalem, and he is also aware that he may be in physical danger from the hostile and unbelieving Jewish leaders there (15:31). Consequently, he makes his second request as he asks them to "strive together with me in your prayers to God for me" (15:30, KJV). Their prayer support was needed in this next leg of his journey.

Here then is the "proof of the pudding." Paul's understanding of what God has done in Jesus Christ was not just a lofty theology to be reflected on in some ivory tower. Instead, it compelled him to go to the ends of the earth to share with people everywhere the Good News of the transformation that God could bring about in their lives. Moreover, his understanding of that inclusive gospel drove him, a Jew, to devote his life's work to working with non-Jews. The racial and religious prejudice from his own background had been replaced by a love that knew no physical limits. He loved, accepted, and devoted himself to the winning of the Gentiles to Christ, even if it meant being ostracized by his fellow Jews.

Furthermore, his call for unity between Jews and Gentiles within the body of Christ was not mere idle words of advice. He was not just writing about what *others* should do; he was putting his words into action, even at the cost of postponing or jeopardizing his own wants and desires. And if it involved the risk of rejection and even physical harm, he was determined to go to Jerusalem to do what he could to bring unity and peace between Jews and non-Jews within the church.

Paul practiced what he preached! He gives us in words and actions a model of faith at work that is sorely needed in our world today.

Personal Greetings

For some students of the New Testament, Romans 16 doesn't seem to fit. Chapter 15 ended with a benediction, "Now the God of peace be with you all. Amen" (15:33, KJV). It would appear this was the logical ending to the letter. But now he seems to go on, naming a long list of people to whom he sends personal greetings.

Two questions arise. How could he have known personally so many people in a church that he had neither founded nor visited? Then, too, some of the names mentioned seem misplaced. Priscilla and Aquila (16:3), according to the Acts story, were last seen in Ephesus, not Rome (Acts 18:24 and following). And Epenetus (spelled Epaenetus in some Bible translations), the first convert in Asia (16:5), would not be expected to be seen in Rome.

Because of these questions, some Bible students have concluded that this chapter was not originally a part of this letter, but many Bible experts argue that the chapter does belong to the epistle, rather than being a fragment of some other document that came to be added to Romans. There are several reasons for believing this.

First, it seems unlikely Paul would know so many people in Rome. Travel was not uncommon in the first century, and the capital of the empire would attract people from all over the Mediterranean. This certainly could be true of Epenetus, who, though converted in the province of Asia, could easily have relocated within the Roman Empire.

Second, Paul would be especially careful to name as many people as possible in his letter. If this is in fact a letter requesting prayer as well as financial support, then it would be to Paul's advantage to indicate how many people within the group he has known previously. They could vouch for his credibility and even put their "stamp of approval" upon his requests.

Third, it is possible that Aquila and Priscilla *were* in Rome. Earlier, they had been forced to leave there for Corinth during the reign of Claudius (Acts 18:2). Would it be unlikely, then, that they would return after Claudius had been succeeded by Nero?

Finally, one other fact that really tips the scale is the appearance of the name Rufus (16:13). In only one other place in the New Testament is someone by this name mentioned. In Mark 15:21 we are told that Simon of Cyrene, who carried the cross for Jesus, was the father of Alexander and Rufus. Why would Mark be the only Gospel writer to mention these names? A likely answer is, Mark mentions them because they are known by the first readers of Mark's Gospel, and the earliest tradition places the writing of this Gospel in Rome. Although we can't prove that the Rufus mentioned in the Gospel of Mark is the same person mentioned in the epistle to the Romans, it seems more than a mere coincidence that the name is mentioned just two times—once in a Roman Gospel and the other time in the Roman letter.

Commendation of Phoebe

The chapter begins (16:1–2) with a word of commendation for Phoebe, who ministered in the church at Cenchreae, the port of Corinth. The word used to describe her is translated "servant" in the King James Version, among others. The word is the one from which we derive our English word *deacon*, which is how the New International Version translates it. There is no feminine form of the word; Phoebe is simply called a servant or a deacon of that particular church. Paul commends her to the Roman Christians, asking that they welcome her, for she has been a helper to him and many other believers (16:2). It is also probable that she is the person who is delivering this letter for Paul.

Greetings from Paul

The names of the people to whom Paul sends greetings give some insight into the composition of the church in Rome and into the ministry of Paul (16:3–16). For example, some mentioned are Jews (Priscilla and Aquila, verse 3; Paul's kinsmen, Andronicus and Junia, verse 7; and Herodion, verse 11). Certain other names indicate a Gentile background (Narcissus, verse 11; Hermes, verse 14; and Olympas, verse 15).

Some of those mentioned had been Paul's fellow prisoners (verse 7); many had a close working relationship with him (verses 3–4). There is even one, the mother of Rufus, who has also been like a mother to Paul (verse 13). The prominence of several women indicates the importance conferred upon women in the first-century churches.

The Christians in Rome who are best known are Priscilla and her husband, Aquila (16:3). Paul had lived and worked with them in Corinth and then had taken them with him to Ephesus (Acts 18). The incident in which they risked their lives for Paul is not otherwise known, but it does indicate the depth of the long and loving relationship Paul had enjoyed with this couple.

Greetings are also sent to "the church that meets at their house" (16:5, NIV). Because of our identification of churches with buildings, we sometimes fail to realize that church buildings as separate, single-purpose, standalone structures were not generally built until the fourth century. Congregations normally met in the homes of church members.

Verse 5 also tells us something about the church at Rome. The one church there included several congregations. There was no one place to which they had access where they could all meet together.

After listing all of these people, Paul encouraged them to "greet one another with a holy kiss" (16:16, NASB). Infrequently practiced in Western churches, this ancient Christian form of greeting is still featured in the worship of Eastern Orthodox Christians.

A Final Admonition

Although they are to greet one another with the holy kiss, there is one group that the Roman Christians are advised to avoid: those who create dissensions and who teach false doctrines (16:17). Troublemakers and smooth talkers who spread and teach untruth and who are concerned only with their own interests have always been used by Satan to deceive unsuspecting people and spread trouble and division in the church (16:17–20). They were present in the church at Rome, even as they are still present in the church today.

Greetings from Paul's Associates

The names of those who sent greetings to the Christians in Rome are similar to those to whom greetings were sent (16:21–23). Paul has with him fellow Jewish Christians (16:21) and some with a definite Gentile background (16:22–23).

Tertius and Quartus ("Third" and "Fourth"), for example, are typical of the numbers given as names to Roman sons.

Again, the first name mentioned, Timothy, is the one best known. This young man from Lystra had joined Paul on the second missionary journey (Acts 16) and became the apostle's closest companion.

Tertius identifies himself as the writer of the letter (16:22). It was Paul's custom to dictate his letters, and from this we learn that Tertius was the secretary for the epistle to Romans.

The names of Gaius and Erastus (16:23) are also interesting. Gaius, Paul's host, may be the same person mentioned in 1 Corinthians 1:14. Such a greeting lends credence to the idea that Romans was written from Corinth. The mention of Erastus, the "chamberlain of the city," indicates that Christians came from all walks of life. Not only were there slaves and tradesmen; Erastus was a city official.

The Closing Doxology

With the greetings complete, Paul now closes the letter with a hymn of praise to God (16:25–27). At several points in these last two chapters of Romans, Paul has written benedictions that might lead the reader to think that the letter is ending (15:5–6, 13, 33; 16:20, 24). But in each case, he has continued. Here, though, he does reach his conclusion, and in it he summarizes the gospel he has developed throughout the epistle.

In this summary, Paul alludes again to Jews and Gentiles and their salvation. The mystery or plan of God that was hidden for ages has been revealed to all the Gentiles ("all nations"—verse 26, ESV) in the prophetic writings of the

Jews as now understood in the light of the gospel. This all-encompassing plan of God is to bring about, in Jew and Gentile alike, the obedience of faith—the obedience that faith engenders in response to the grace of God. For this obedience of faith, Paul has been called (1:5). Concerning this obedience of faith, he has written to the Romans. Because of this obedience of faith, he gives praise "to the only wise God be glory forever through Jesus Christ! Amen" (16:27, NIV).

To this obedience of faith, Paul continues to call us as Christians today. Even though our world is quite different from that of Paul and his first-century readers, the message that he wrote to them still strikes a responsive chord in us.

To be sure, the Christian faith that Paul shared with the church in Rome through this letter is still our faith. Like the Christians of the first century, we believe that sinful humanity is in need of salvation and that God has provided for this need in Jesus Christ. And we affirm, as did Paul, that a person becomes a participant in this salvation process only through faith—that by our faith and trust in Christ, we are put into right relationship with God. We affirm, also, with Paul that everyone who experiences this salvation is to give witness to it in Christian behavior.

At this point, perhaps, Paul's letter speaks most forthrightly to us. The problem of a church divided is still our problem. Tensions that existed between members of the same congregation then are also prevalent today.

Like the Christians in Rome, we need to hear again Paul's words of advice about love and acceptance of one another.

We need to learn from his words of guidance about living as Christians in a non-Christian world.

As long as we Christians strive to maintain our unity and our identity in a hostile environment, and as long as we feel the need to examine and reflect on the fundamental facets of our faith, we can continue to learn from the epistle of Paul to the Romans.

━━━━━━━━━━━━━━━━━━━━━━

God, I rejoice in what I've learned in these lessons. Help me apply these truths to my daily life. AMEN.

May the God of endurance and encouragement grant you to live in such harmony with one another, in accord with Christ Jesus, that together you may with one voice glorify the God and Father of our Lord Jesus Christ.

—Romans 15:5–6 (ESV)

I love to sing, especially in parts. Years ago I sang in a gospel quartet, and I sing tenor in the church choir. My voice isn't beautiful, but I can hit the right notes. Once I know them.

You see, I'm not very good at reading music. My musical friends sight-read. They look at the written music and hear the song in their heads. I don't. I need to hear the starting note or I'm halfway through the verse before I find the harmony. I do even better if the accompanist plunks out my part. Sometimes I ask her to play a particularly difficult interval over and over while I match pitches. I drum it into my head all week long and by Sunday I can sing it easily, able to pay attention to the director and the dynamics.

In one sense, written music is the song. If you purchase the sheet music to Handel's *Messiah*, you hold it in your hands. But that isn't all it was designed to be. The *Messiah* is meant to be experienced in a candlelit cathedral where beautiful voices lift the listeners to a place the score could never take them. So, too, God's written Word is complete, strong, and sufficient to achieve His purposes. But it is intended to be more—something seen and heard, more than words on paper or concepts in our minds. His Word is meant to work in us, capture our hearts, and transform us so that our changed lives, impossible to hide, are experienced by an audience who'll see Jesus in our attitudes and actions even if they've never read the Word at all.

—*Suzanne Davenport Tietjen*

Notes

Notes

Notes

_____

_____

_____

_____

_____

_____

_____

_____

_____

_____

_____

_____

_____

_____

_____

_____

_____

_____

_____

_____

Acknowledgments

Every attempt has been made to credit the sources of copyrighted material used in this book. If any such acknowledgment has been inadvertently omitted or miscredited, receipt of such information would be appreciated.

Scripture quotations marked (AMP) are taken from the *Amplified Bible*. Copyright © 2015 by The Lockman Foundation, La Habra, California. All rights reserved.

Scripture quotations marked (ESV) are taken from *The Holy Bible, English Standard Version*. Copyright © 2001 by Crossway Bibles, a division of Good News Publishers. Used by permission. All rights reserved.

Scripture quotations marked (KJV) are taken from the *King James Version of the Bible*.

Scripture quotations marked (NASB) are taken from the *New American Standard Bible*®. Copyright © 1960, 1971, 1977, 1995, 2020 by The Lockman Foundation. All rights reserved.

Scripture quotations marked (NIV) are taken from *The Holy Bible, New International Version*®, *NIV*®. Copyright © 1973, 1978, 1984, 2011 by Biblica, Inc. Used by permission. All rights reserved worldwide.

Scripture quotations marked (NLT) are taken from *Holy Bible, New Living Translation*. Copyright © 1996, 2004, 2015 by Tyndale House Foundation. Used by permission of Tyndale House Publishers, Inc., Carol Stream, Illinois 60188. All rights reserved.

A Note from the Editors

◆―――――――――――――――――――◆

We hope you enjoyed *Living with Purpose Bible Study: Romans* published by Guideposts. For over 75 years, Guideposts, a nonprofit organization, has been driven by a vision of a world filled with hope. We aspire to be the voice of a trusted friend, a friend who makes you feel more hopeful and connected.

By making a purchase from Guideposts, you join our community in touching millions of lives, inspiring them to believe that all things are possible through faith, hope, and prayer. Your continued support allows us to provide uplifting resources to those in need. Whether through our communities, websites, apps, or publications, we inspire our audiences, bring them together, and comfort, uplift, entertain, and guide them. Visit us at guideposts.org to learn more.

We would love to hear from you. Write us at Guideposts, P.O. Box 5815, Harlan, Iowa 51593 or call us at (800) 932-2145. Did you love *Living with Purpose Bible Study: Romans*? Leave a review for this product on guideposts.org/shop. Your feedback helps others in our community find relevant products.

Find inspiration, find faith, find Guideposts.

Shop our best sellers and favorites at
guideposts.org/shop

Or scan the QR code to go directly to our Shop